Biographies

PATRICIA LAUBER, formerly editor-in-chief of a young people's science magazine and Chief Editor, Science and Mathematics, for a leading children's encyclopedia, is the author of some 40 books, many concerning science. She has contributed titles to three other Random House series. A graduate of Wellesley College, she now lives in New York City.

JOHN POLGREEN has illustrated many science books, including several for the Random House Look-It-Up series. He is an active member of the Association of Lunar and Planetary Observers and of the American Association of Variable Star Observers. In collaboration with his wife, Cathleen, who is also an enthusiastic amateur astronomer, he wrote and illustrated *The Earth in Space*. The Polgreens live in Dobbs Ferry, New York.

Cover photograph: The planet Saturn and its rings as seen through the 120-inch telescope of the Lick Observatory in California.

The Planets

Hope you enjoy this book and learn a lot of important things.
— Mama "J"

Random House Science Library Advisory Board

Robert E. Dearen
Consultant
Palm Beach County Board of
   Public Instruction, Florida

Sanford M. Eisler
Directing Supervisor of Science
Cleveland Public Schools

Keith C. Johnson
Supervising Director, Department of Science
Public Schools of the District of Columbia

Samuel S. Lepow
Director of Science Education
The School District of Philadelphia

Dallas W. Maddron
Science Supervisor
The Board of Public Instruction
   for the County of Orange, Florida

Samuel Schenberg
Director of Science
Board of Education of the City of New York

Richard W. Schulz
Consultant, Science and Mathematics
Cedar Rapids Community School District

The Planets

by Patricia Lauber
illustrated by John Polgreen

RANDOM HOUSE SCIENCE LIBRARY
RANDOM HOUSE · NEW YORK

The photographs in this book are reproduced through the courtesy of: Cover: Lick Observatory; American Museum of Natural History: 41; Central Office of Information, London: 30; Lick Observatory: 74, 101; Lowell Observatory Photograph: 50, 54–55, 64–65, 69, 90, 94, 96, 107; Mount Wilson and Palomar: vi, 29, 33, 34 (all), 38 (top), 58–59, 62, 70, 88, 126–127; NASA: 5, 43, 44–45, 75, 76; Ronan Picture Library: 16, 21, 67; Yerkes Observatory Photograph: 11, 38 (bottom), 81, 91, 98, 104.

Contents

1

The Cloud

Long, long ago a vast cloud floated in space. It was big beyond imagining, probably trillions of miles in diameter, and it was made of gas and dust. In the beginning, the tiny particles that composed the cloud were spread very thin.

As the cloud floated, it kept drawing in material from neighboring space. Its mass (the amount of material in it) grew and grew. The particles tended to attract one another. They moved closer together, and so the cloud became more dense. As a result, gravity became stronger, pulling the dust and gas toward the center of the cloud. The cloud began to contract.

Over millions of years, material streamed inward toward the center of the cloud. It streamed faster and faster until the cloud collapsed in on itself, forming a huge ball of gas and dust. The ball began to spin.

The Lagoon Nebula in Sagittarius

In time the spinning caused the ball to flatten into a giant disk. The disk was thickest in the middle, and it thinned out toward the edges.

The middle, which was spinning more slowly than the edges, condensed into a huge mass of gas and dust. The particles in it were under very great pressure. The temperature rose until the mass became white-hot. It began to glow and to give off heat and light. In this way, a new **star** was born. It was the star that men would one day call their sun.

Meanwhile, the outer parts of the disk had broken up into swirling eddies of gas and dust. The dust particles, which were heavier, settled toward the centers of the eddies. Small particles collided with larger particles and were added to the bodies of the larger ones. The collisions created heat. At the heart of the eddies, masses of glowing-hot material took shape. Some swept up other masses, growing larger and larger.

As time passed, the largest eddies condensed into the bodies that we call the **planets.** Some smaller eddies condensed into **moons.**

2

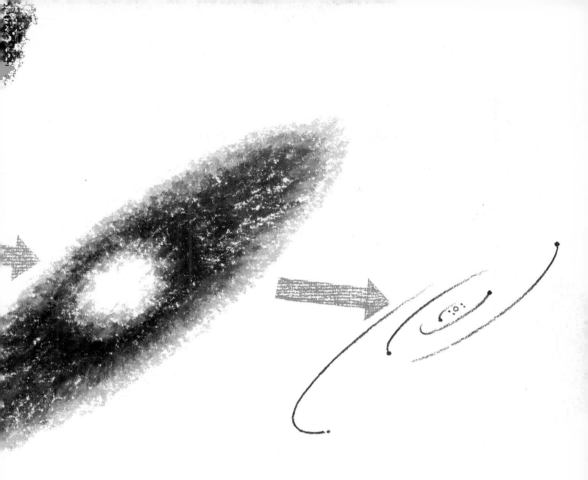

In much this way, most scientists think, our **solar system** came into being almost five billion years ago. The **sun** was born of a cloud of gas and dust. The planets formed out of the same material.

When this first stage ended, the newly formed planets were swinging around the newly glowing sun in widely spaced **orbits.** Some were only millions of miles from the sun. Others were several billion miles away, out where the edge of the great disk had been.

Perhaps at that time the planets all looked very much alike. And in many ways they were alike. Yet one planet—the third one out from the sun—turned out to be different. This was the planet Earth, which long after became our home.

3

2

Earth, Our Home Planet

Seen from far out in space, Earth is simply a fairly small planet that shines with a fairly bright light. There is nothing very eye-catching about it. It isn't a brilliant giant, like Jupiter. It isn't circled by beautiful rings, like Saturn. It isn't red like Mars. It has only one moon, compared with Jupiter's twelve or Saturn's ten.

Yet a closer view of the earth, say, from its moon, shows a very interesting planet. The earth is marked with brilliant white patches—its polar icecaps and its clouds. Continents are outlined against oceans.

A really close view shows that the earth is the loveliest and most interesting planet in the solar system. For the earth is a planet of life.

The continents, rising out of the oceans, are clothed in the greens of forests and grasslands. Over a period of months the greens change. Pale greens darken, then turn yellow or red-brown. For a few months some greens vanish. An area that was green appears brown-gray or white. Then once more pale greens appear and darken.

4

The earth, photographed by Lunar Orbiter V *from over 200,000 miles away*

EARTH

average diameter	7,913 miles
average distance from sun	92,900,000 miles
average speed of revolution	67,000 miles per hour
length of year	365¼ days
length of day	23 hours, 56 minutes
number of moons	1

These changing colors are a sign of widespread, vigorous plant life. This fact alone makes Earth a remarkable planet. But there is something else that shows the earth to be very remarkable indeed. When the shadows of night fall upon certain parts of the earth, the lights of great cities go on. This is a sign of intelligent life, and it makes the earth unique. No other planet in our solar system shows signs of supporting intelligent life.

The planet Earth is basically nothing more than a ball of rock covered mostly by water and surrounded by an envelope of air. Spinning on its **axis**, the earth revolves around the sun at 67,000 miles an hour.

Yet there are many things about this small planet that make it just right for supporting life.

To start with, there is the sun we circle. Compared with other stars, our sun is not particularly big or brilliant. But from our point of view, it is exceptionally fine.

Our sun is a steady producer of the light and heat required by life on Earth. Many stars are not such steady producers of light and heat. Some change often, dimming and then growing brighter. Some flare up suddenly, turning loose a blast of withering heat. Our sun does none of these things. Its output of light and heat hardly varies at all.

Our sun's gravitational field is also steady. It keeps the earth orbiting steadily around the sun. If the sun's gravitational field were not steady, the earth might be tossed about like a ping-pong ball on a stormy sea. Sometimes it would be pulled too close

6

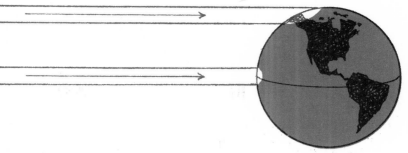

to the sun. At other times it would be too far away. Great changes in climate would occur each time the distance changed. This would make many, and perhaps all, kinds of life impossible. Living things depend on a regular climate.

Earth's distance from the sun is also ideal. On the average, the earth is about 93 million miles from the sun. It receives just the right amount of heat and light to support our kind of life.

The way our planet moves around the sun is also very important to life.

As it **revolves** around the sun, the earth is also **rotating**. That is, it spins on its axis, an imaginary line running through the North and South Poles. It completes one spin in just a little less than 24 hours. By the time the earth has made 365 rotations, it has completed one trip around the sun. As we see it, the sun has risen and set 365 times, and so we say that a year has 365 days.

The year also has seasons. The seasons result from the tilt of the earth's axis. Each pole is tipped toward the sun for part of the year. The Northern Hemisphere has summer when the North Pole is tipped toward the sun. It has winter when the North Pole is tipped away.

Earth's spin and the tilt of its axis make our planet an extremely pleasant place to live. Every part of the earth gets some sunlight. Only the polar regions are very cold. Only the regions around the equator are very hot. Most parts of the earth are kept at bearable temperatures. The seasons change, and different parts of the earth become warmer or cooler. In the

When the North Pole is tilted away from the sun, it is winter in the Northern Hemisphere. Then the sun's rays reach the ground at a slant and are more spread out. Also, the sun shines for fewer hours each day so that the weaker rays do not have as much time to heat up the earth.

7

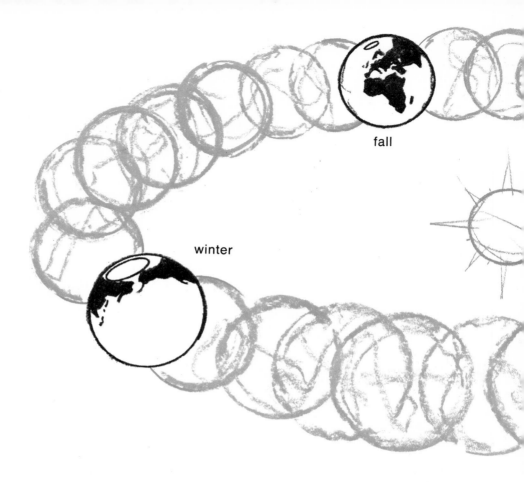

fall

winter

same way, day brings warmth and night brings a cooling-off.

Our planet has other good things about it, too. One of the most important is the **atmosphere**, the blanket of air several hundred miles deep that surrounds the earth.

We could not live without the atmosphere. It is the air we breathe. It is a shield, filtering out dangerous rays from the sun. It is a blanket that traps part of the day's heat from the sun and keeps the heat from escaping at night.

The atmosphere is held captive by the earth's **gravity.** Its gravity is another thing that is just right about the earth. The strength of gravity is determined by a body's mass. The moon, for example, has less

8

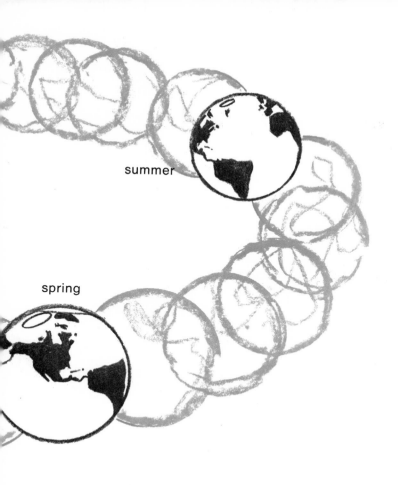

Seasons in the Northern Hemisphere

mass than the earth and its pull of gravity is about one sixth of the earth's; the moon cannot hold an atmosphere. Jupiter, on the other hand, has more mass than the earth and its pull of gravity is about two and a half times as strong; Jupiter holds a very dense atmosphere thousands of miles deep. Earth's gravity is strong enough to hold an atmosphere. But it holds a relatively thin atmosphere that light can pass through.

The mixture of gases in Earth's atmosphere is good, too. The mixture is about four-fifths nitrogen and one-fifth oxygen, with traces of argon, carbon dioxide, helium, hydrogen, and several other gases. The carbon dioxide is required by plants. The oxygen —called "free oxygen" because it is not combined

9

with other elements—is what men and animals require. To the best of our knowledge, there is not much free oxygen on any planet except Earth.

So in every way—its steady sun, its regular orbit, its distance from the sun, its seasons, its short days and nights, its atmosphere—Earth is, for us, the most pleasant planet imaginable. It is the only one in our solar system that could support our kind of life.

In a way, of course, this would have to be so. Since life evolved here, it's only natural that the earth seems ideal to us. And we can go one step further. It is also true that part of the earth's pleasantness has been created by the living things that developed here. For the earth as we know it today did not spring into existence ready-made.

Nobody knows what the earth was like at the time of its birth four or five billion years ago. But many scientists think that it was wrapped in a dense cloud of atmosphere, which was later driven away by

10

radiation from the sun. Underneath this ball of clouds the young earth was extremely hot. It may have been so hot that the solid material took the form of gas. After a while the earth began to cool. The gases condensed into liquid, turning the earth into a mass of seething lava. The heavier elements (iron and nickel) settled toward the center of the mass, forming the molten outer core that the earth still has.

The earth went on cooling. For hundreds of millions of years it bubbled and gave off gases. In time a thin, solid crust began to form on the young and cooling earth. Lava flowed from cracks in the crust, bringing steam to the surface. The steam rose into the atmosphere.

At some time during the cooling-off, the air temperature dropped to a point where rain occurred. It was rain that fell only in the sky. When raindrops neared the earth's cooling but still hot crust, they

The Arizona meteorite crater. When the earth was young, it was blasted by huge meteorites: rocks and other debris from space. Today these huge objects are gone, but smaller ones still exist. They range in size from specks of dust to big rocks. Many enter the earth's atmosphere, where the heat of friction usually turns them to vapor. Only a few are so big that they reach the earth's surface without being wholly vaporized. The name for any of these objects that enter the atmosphere is meteoroid. The flash of light that a meteoroid makes in the night sky is called a meteor. A meteoroid that reaches our planet's surface is called a meteorite.

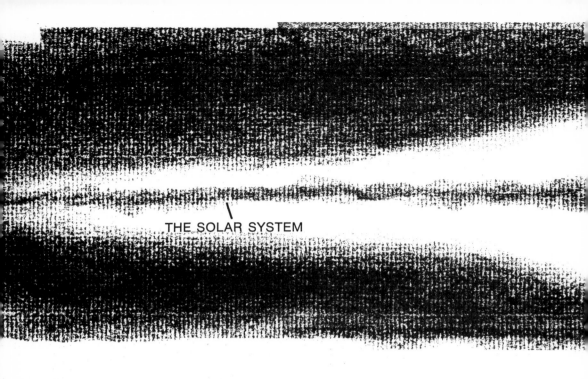

THE SOLAR SYSTEM

A side view of the Milky Way as it would appear to an observer in space

evaporated. Steam rose into the atmosphere, condensed, and turned again to rain. Only when the crust cooled still more did the first rains strike the earth's surface. Over a long period of time, rain fell in a steady deluge. The wrinkled areas in the crust filled with water, and so the first oceans formed.

By the time it was two billion years old, the earth had changed greatly.

It now had a cool, solid crust. Most of the crust was probably covered by oceans. Land areas—if there were any—consisted of rock. The soil lying in cracks between the rocks was ground-up stone. The oceans, the rocks, the soil were all barren and lifeless.

Surrounding the earth was an atmosphere of poisonous gases. Most likely they included ammonia and methane. The ammonia was a compound of nitrogen and hydrogen. The methane was a compound of carbon and hydrogen.

By this time the atmosphere was thin enough so that some sunlight could penetrate it and reach the surface of the earth. The sunlight fell upon scenes of

12

terrible violence. The earth was still growing, catching up material from space. Giant **meteorites** pelted the young planet, blasting craters in its crust. Thunderstorms raged across the surface. Volcanoes exploded. Mighty forces deep within the earth squeezed and folded the surface, forcing up mountains.

That scene set the stage for life.

Modern scientists believe that life will appear wherever conditions remain favorable for a very long time. And they say that conditions on the earth two billion years ago were just right for life to begin.

Scientists do not know, and may never know, precisely how life began. But they suppose that something like this may have happened.

Heat and lightning acted on certain gases in the atmosphere, creating amino acids, which are the building blocks of living matter. The amino acids were carried by raindrops into the warm ocean. In time they combined into more complex structures. Then—somewhere, somehow, sometime—a piece of living protein was produced.

13

What happened after that is a whole story in itself. For our purposes, it is enough to know that in the lifeless ocean of the young earth, life was probably born. From that first life all other life is descended.

The development of the first living molecule may have taken a few million years or a billion years or even more. The earliest living molecules may have continued in the same form for a billion years, or only a few million. But eventually a great change took place.

A molecule began to capture energy from sunlight. It used the energy to make food out of chemicals. The process of using sunlight to make food is called photosynthesis, and it is the way most modern plants make their food.

The first plants were probably tiny and slow-growing, though this is just a guess. We can be sure of only one thing about them. The most successful ones became the ancestors of our green plants; they established the pattern of plant life we know today. The plants absorbed carbon dioxide, a compound of carbon and oxygen. They absorbed water, a compound of hydrogen and oxygen. From these two compounds the plants drew carbon and hydrogen. They released the oxygen. The oxygen was drawn into the atmosphere.

The new, food-making plants multiplied and spread. Day after day, they took in carbon dioxide and water, used the carbon and hydrogen, and released free oxygen. As a result, the atmosphere very slowly began to change. The amount of free oxygen in it increased. And oxygen is chemically very active.

Oxygen attacked the methane in the air, changing

14

it to carbon dioxide and water. Oxygen attacked ammonia, combining with the hydrogen in it to form water and releasing the nitrogen. After a while, there were no more gases for the oxygen to attack. It simply began to accumulate in the atmosphere.

The atmosphere became much like today's atmosphere—chiefly a mixture of nitrogen and oxygen, with just a trace of carbon dioxide and other gases. Then another great change took place. The animal age began.

The first animals did not even vaguely resemble dogs or horses or tigers. Like the early plants, they were just large molecules. The chief difference between them and the plants was the way each group made food.

The plants drew energy from sunlight, broke down carbon dioxide, and used the carbon. They released the oxygen into the air.

The animals ate plants and used oxygen to "burn" their food. They gave off carbon dioxide into the air.

Animal life today, including man, still does precisely that. All animal life depends on green plants. The plants are food; the oxygen freed by plants is the fuel needed to "burn" the food.

So, out of the young earth's atmosphere and seas came life. Plant life changed the atmosphere. Animal life began. Plants and animals changed the land as they learned to live on it. Higher forms of life developed from lower ones. Earth became more and more the world we know today—a small but remarkable planet which is our home and from which we look out into the sky, seeking to know what lies beyond us.

15

A Ptolemaic map of the heavens, centered on the earth. From Peter Apian's Cosmographia, *1539. The legend around the outside reads "The empyrian heaven, dwelling of God and all the saints."*

3

The Five Wanderers

Probably from earliest times men turned their eyes upward with awe, marveling at the sun that filled the sky by day and the stars that came by night. Then, watching and remembering, they realized that there was a regularity to what happened in the heavens. They began to make use of this. They used the sun and stars as guides to direction. The phases of the moon helped them keep track of passing time. So did the appearance of certain **constellations,** which foretold the coming of the seasons. Thus at some time long ago the oldest of sciences, **astronomy**, was born out of a need to know the skies.

As ancient astronomers mapped the night skies, they found five stars that were strangely different from the others.

17

Most stars always held the same position in the same constellation; they appeared to be fixed in place. The five did not. Instead, they wandered through a certain band of constellations. They were different in one other way, too. While the fixed stars shone with a twinkling light, the five shone with a light that was steadier.

The ancient Greeks, the world's first great scientists, gave the five strange stars a special name. The name meant wanderers, and from it has come our word planets. The five wandering stars of old were the planets that we call Mercury, Venus, Mars, Jupiter, and Saturn.

The Greeks carefully plotted the paths of the planets through the night sky. The results posed a very great problem. The planets would not fit into the system that astronomers used to explain the workings of the **universe**.

The ancients believed that the earth stood still, while all the heavenly bodies revolved around it. Their reasoning is not hard to understand. Why should anyone think that this solid, stable earth was moving? Here it was—the same, day after day, beneath men's feet. On the other hand, anyone could see that the sun, the moon, and the stars were all moving. At various rates, they traveled across the sky, vanished, and returned. Clearly, the earth stood still and all things moved around it.

Astronomers explained that the universe consisted of a series of crystal spheres, one within another. At the center of the spheres was the earth. Beyond it, each in a separate sphere, lay the moon, Mercury, Venus, the sun, Mars, Jupiter, and Saturn. Beyond

18

these lay a large, dark sphere to which the stars were fixed. All the spheres revolved around the earth.

The system worked quite well for the moon, the sun, and the stars. All of them appeared regularly and moved regularly across the sky. But it did not work for the planets. Instead of moving steadily forward, the wanderers sometimes reversed their courses and moved backward for a short time. How could this happen if each planet was attached to a perfectly round sphere and circling the earth?

One of the astronomers who attacked this problem was Ptolemy of Alexandria. He explained the motions of the planets this way. Each planet, he said, is moving around the earth in the circle of its sphere. But each planet also has a second motion. It is moving in a small circle that lies on the edge of the large circle. That is, the planet is moving around the circumference of a small circle; the center of the small circle moves around the circumference of the large circle.

There the matter rested for more than a thousand years. The great age of learning had come to an end and was not reborn until the 1200's.

At that time manuscripts from the ancient world found their way into the hands of Church scholars in Europe. The scholars were stunned by the wealth of information in these books. With great enthusiasm they took over the scientific ideas of Greece and Alexandria, including the belief that the earth was the center of the universe. It was an extremely pleasing idea. For if the earth was the center of the universe and man was master of the earth, then man was master of the universe.

19

Astronomers, however, were still faced with the problem of explaining the motions of the planets.

They observed that the planets did not always move at the same speed. How could this be so if they were all moving around the earth in perfect circles? Astronomers tried to solve the problem by giving the earth a position slightly off center in their diagrams. If the earth was not at the exact center of the universe, then the speed of the planets would appear to vary.

A still worse problem was the one Ptolemy had attacked. Usually the planets are seen moving eastward among the stars. Yet the time comes when a planet seems to turn around and move westward. How could this be explained?

Astronomers adopted Ptolemy's solution. But careful observation kept turning up things that couldn't be explained by a small circle on a large circle. So astronomers kept adding more circles. Finally they had a collection of circles upon circles upon circles. And it still didn't explain the motions of the planets.

The man who cut through this problem was the Polish astronomer Copernicus. He worked out a new system, which placed the sun at the center of the universe.

This was a daring idea. At the time, an attack on an earth-centered universe was considered an attack on the Church. So Copernicus hesitated to publish his theory. Instead he made it part of a long and technical book, which was published in 1543. Buried in the book were three very important ideas:

20

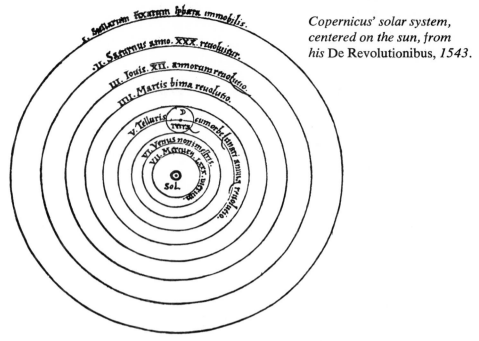

Copernicus' solar system, centered on the sun, from his De Revolutionibus, *1543.*

First, the sun, not the earth, is the center of the universe. Second, all the planets, including the earth, move around the sun. Third, Earth spins on its axis once every 24 hours; it is the earth's rotation that makes the sun and stars appear to move around us.

These ideas helped to explain the strange wanderings of the planets. Mars, for example, does not really move backward. It just appears to because both the earth and Mars are moving. When the earth overtakes Mars, Mars seems to move backward.

Among the people who read Copernicus' book were two great astronomers, the Italian Galileo and the German Johannes Kepler. Galileo struck the next blow for a sun-centered universe.

In 1609 Galileo heard that a Dutch spectacles-maker had accidentally invented a spyglass. Galileo immediately set about building one for himself. In the winter of 1609-10 he became the first man to turn a **telescope** on the night sky.

The moon, the stars, the planets—there was so

21

much to see that Galileo hardly knew how to spend his time. He noted a difference in the appearance of the planets and the stars. The planets, he reported, "show their globes perfectly round . . . looking like little moons, spherical and flooded all over with light. The fixed stars . . . have the aspect of blazes whose rays vibrate about them."

Turning his telescope on Jupiter, he discovered that the planet had moons revolving around it. Here before his eyes was a miniature solar system. The moons revolved around Jupiter just as Copernicus had said the planets revolve around the sun.

The telescope showed Galileo that Venus went through **phases**, like the moon. This was further evidence that Copernicus was right. The phases could occur only if Venus was moving around the sun and was closer than Earth to the sun.

Galileo's findings caused a tremendous uproar and got him into serious trouble. But the truth about man's place in the universe was beginning to emerge. Once started, it could not be stopped.

Just about that time, Kepler announced the first of his three great laws that explain the movement of the planets about the sun. Kepler destroyed the old and false idea that planets move in circles. He showed that planets move in ellipses. He also proved that the speed of a planet does vary. As a planet nears the sun, it speeds up; as it draws away from the sun, it slows down.

And some years later, Isaac Newton explained why planets travel around the sun in orbits.

Part of the explanation is found in Newton's first law of motion. It says that an object in motion (or at

22

rest) tends to remain in that state unless acted upon by an outside force. That is, a ball lying on a tennis court tends to remain at rest. It will not move unless acted upon by an outside force, such as the wind or your hand. Set in motion, the ball rolls until it is stopped by an outside force, usually friction with the ground. This tendency to remain in motion (or at rest) is called **inertia**.

A planet is spinning through space. There is no friction to stop it. Nothing lies in its way. It would travel on and on in a straight line, except for the sun's gravity.

The sun's gravity and the planet's inertia work together. Without the sun's pull, the planet would spin off into space. Without inertia, it would be drawn into the fiery mass of the sun. Together the two keep the planet moving around the sun in its orbit.

The work of Copernicus, Galileo, Kepler, and Newton marked the start of modern astronomy. Copernicus and Galileo led the way in showing that man is not the center of the universe or even of the solar system. Kepler and Newton discovered the basic laws that govern the movements of the planets. Once this groundwork had been laid, discoveries came at a staggering rate.

Today we know that the universe extends far beyond what man can see. It is made up of millions of **galaxies**—huge islands of stars. Our sun, far from being the center of the universe, is one star among the billions of stars in our own galaxy.

We also know that our solar system contains nine planets that whirl through space around the sun. A planet is not, as the ancients thought, a kind of wan-

PLUTO

NEPTUNE URAN

dering star. A star is a fiery furnace of gases that generates light and heat. A planet is a much smaller body held captive by a star. It does not generate light and heat. It shines because it is reflecting the star's light. When a planet is far from its star, it cannot reflect much light because it does not receive much. That is why the outer planets are dim. They are not nearly so bright as a much more distant star, which generates its own light.

Today, too, everyone knows that the earth is a planet. It is special because it supports human life. But in every other way it is simply one of nine planets that orbit the sun.

The solar system is a very orderly place. As seen from the north side, the sun spins on its axis in a counter-clockwise direction. That is the general direction of movement in the solar system. Most of the planets also spin counter-clockwise. All of them move counter-clockwise around the sun. Most moons orbit their planets in a counter-clockwise direction.

Except for Pluto, all the planets move in nearly the same plane in space. That is, their orbits line up.

Every planet's orbit is an ellipse. Some of these orbits come very close to being circles, but they are still ellipses. The planets travel around their orbits at

24

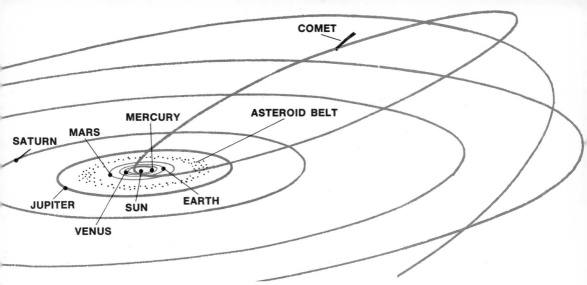

COMET
MERCURY
ASTEROID BELT
MARS
SATURN
JUPITER
SUN
EARTH
VENUS

varying speeds that follow a pattern: the closer a planet is to the sun, the faster it travels.

Astronomers have found that the planets fall into two distinct classes, determined by size and density. Density is a measure of the amount of matter in a body of a certain volume. (A baseball and a tennis ball, for example, are about the same size. But the baseball is much more dense: there is more matter packed into its volume.)

One class consists of small, solid planets—Mercury, Venus, Earth, Mars, and Pluto. Earth is the largest of these. All have an average density several times that of water.

The other class is made up of the giant planets—Jupiter, Saturn, Uranus, Neptune. The largest of these, Jupiter, has a diameter almost eleven times greater than the earth's. Neptune, the smallest, has a diameter three and a half times that of the earth. However, the densities of the four giants are low. So they must be made in part of gas or liquid.

One of the most striking things about our solar system is its "emptiness," the vast gulfs of space that lie between the planets. On the average, Mercury is almost 36 million miles from the sun. Pluto is a hundred times farther away. Between these two are

The solar system, with nine planets revolving around the sun in elliptical orbits.

25

Comet Ikeya-Seki, first seen in 1965 by two Japanese astronomers and named for them

Morehouse's Comet, last seen in 1908

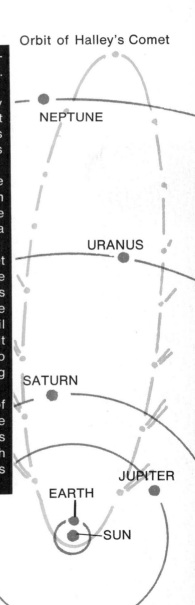

HEAD

TAIL

nucleus coma

Orbit of Halley's Comet

Comets are also members of the solar system, traveling around the sun in huge, sausage-shaped orbits. They seem to be made of dust and frozen gases.

Far from the sun, a comet is something like a big dirty snowball, about half a mile in diameter. It does not glow. Nearing the sun, the comet is warmed, and its outer gases change from ice to vapor. The sun's rays pass through the gases, causing them to glow.

The gases are so light that they are affected by the pressure of the sun's rays. They are pushed away from the sun, and so form a tail. If the comet is very bright, we see it from the earth as a ball-shaped head of light with a long glowing tail.

The tail always points away from the sun. As a comet approaches the sun, the tail streams behind or to one side. As a comet moves away from the sun, the tail goes first. By that time the comet has grown very large. The head may be a million miles in diameter while the tail stretches through millions of miles of space. But as it leaves the sun behind, the comet shrinks and ceases to glow. It becomes again a huge dirty snowball, traveling through space.

On each trip around the sun, a comet loses some of its gas and dust. Finally the comet no longer exists. The gases have escaped into space, but the dust particles continue to orbit the sun. If the earth passes through a swarm of these particles, a meteor shower takes place.

NEPTUNE

URANUS

SATURN

JUPITER

EARTH

SUN

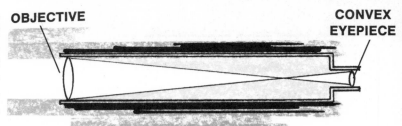

*A simple optical telescope. Light is gathered by the larger lens, or **objective.** The image it makes is magnified by the convex lens of the eyepiece. This type of telescope is called a refractor.*

OBJECTIVE

CONVEX EYEPIECE

PATH OF LIGHT

PRIME FOCUS

the seven other planets. The distances are so great and the planets so small that it is almost impossible to make an accurate model of the solar system. If the earth is made the size of a ping-pong ball, then Pluto must be placed ten miles away.

Even so, astronomers have learned to probe these great distances. They have found planets that are invisible to the unaided eye. They can tell you the the temperatures on Mars. They can tell you about gases in the atmosphere of Venus.

One of the astronomer's most important tools is the **optical telescope.** It gathers light from a distant object, brings light rays together into an image, and then makes the image bigger. In effect, a telescope makes a faraway object look nearer and clearer. It also reveals objects too dim for the unaided eye to see. Astronomers usually couple the telescope with a camera. On light-sensitive plates they record for later study what the telescope "sees."

To measure temperature, astronomers often use a device called a thermocouple, along with a telescope. A highly sensitive thermocouple can detect heat from a candle three miles away.

To analyze light gathered by a telescope, astronomers use a **spectroscope**. It works on this principle. When white light is passed through a **prism**, it spreads out into a rainbow of colors. This band of colors is called a **spectrum** (plural: spectra). Suppose light from a planet or star is passed through a spectroscope. When the colors are widely spread, thousands of lines, both bright and dark, can be seen. Each line has a meaning. For example, a bright yellow-orange line in a certain position shows glowing sodium in

28

The 200-inch Hale reflector telescope at Mount Wilson Observatory, the largest in the world. In a reflector, light is gathered by a large mirror which reflects the image to an observer. Most large telescopes today are reflectors because it is easier to make a high-quality large mirror than a set of large lenses.

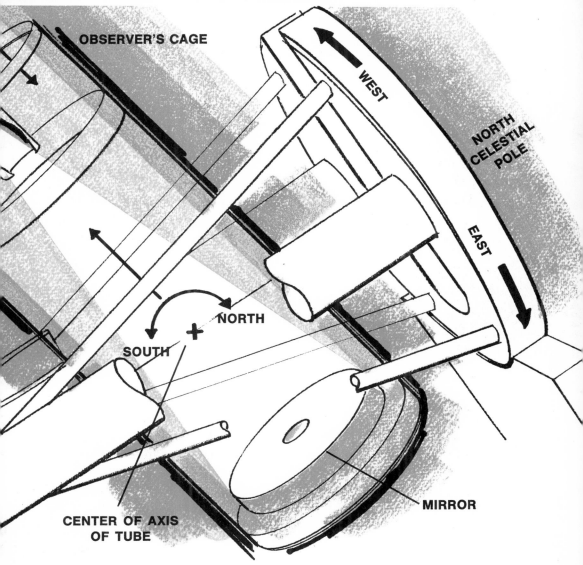

OBSERVER'S CAGE

WEST

NORTH CELESTIAL POLE

EAST

NORTH

SOUTH

MIRROR

CENTER OF AXIS OF TUBE

The Jodrell Bank radio telescope

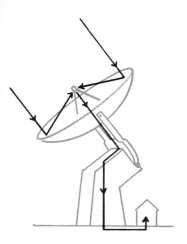

the light source. Other lines show hydrogen, helium, ammonia, and so on. If certain lines are not sharp but fuzzy, they indicate that the planet or star is spinning rapidly.

In recent years astronomers have been using two exciting new tools. One is **radar,** which they use to study nearby bodies such as the moon, the planets, and the sun. A radar set shoots out short bursts of radio waves, called pulses. When the pulses hit an object, they bounce back. The echoes are picked up by a **radar telescope**, which is a big antenna. By timing the echoes astronomers can measure distances accurately. And they can use radar to explore what the eye cannot see. For example, radar pulses have penetrated the thick clouds of Venus and bounced

30

off the planet's surface. A study of the echoes gave astronomers some surprising information about Venus' spin and its surface.

The other new tool is the **radio telescope**, which gathers radio waves given off by distant objects in space as well as nearby objects such as the planets. The study of radio waves from a planet gives clues, for example, to the planet's temperature. These studies have also produced some surprises.

In these ways and others, astronomers have reached out from the earth into space. They have gathered information at a dizzying pace. They have made discoveries undreamed of three centuries ago.

Much of what they have learned about the members of our solar family is summed up in this book. But many tantalizing questions remain without answers because we cannot see well enough. Even the most powerful telescope shows almost nothing of dimly lighted Pluto. It cannot show us what the surface of the moon is made of. And it cannot bring into focus the surface features of Mars.

However, the next great breakthrough in astronomy is under way as rockets and man-made satellites carry the astronomer's instruments into space. Rocket probes and satellites are beginning to supply the answers that long lay just beyond our grasp. And the day is not far distant when men set out in spaceships to explore our neighbors in the solar system. The ancient science of astronomy is about to become a kind of geography as men explore what today we can only imperfectly see. And the first new world to be explored will be the moon, the **satellite** of our planet Earth.

4

The Moon, Earth's Satellite

The moon hangs large in our sky.

It is, to begin with, a very big satellite for a small planet. There are bigger moons in the solar system. But no other moon is so big in proportion to the size of its planet. The moon's diameter is more than a fourth of the earth's.

The moon is also our near neighbor. It is only a quarter of a million miles away, which is very close as distances in the solar system go.

Its size in our sky has always made the moon seem very special to people on Earth. Anyone could see that the moon was big and that it had markings on its face. Many ancient astronomers believed that the markings outlined seas and continents. This suggested that the moon was an inhabited world.

No one today thinks that the moon is inhabited, but it remains very special.

32

EARTH'S MOON

average diameter	2,160 miles
average distance from Earth	238,854.7 miles
period of revolution	$27\frac{1}{3}$ earth days
period of rotation	$27\frac{1}{3}$ earth days
gravity	0.17 of Earth's
surface temperature	$-260°$ F. to $250°$ F.

The moon at (from top to bottom) 3 days, 11 days, 14 days, 20 days, and 26 days

Because it is big and near, astronomers can see it clearly. Since the invention of the telescope, ten generations of them have studied it and thoroughly mapped its face.

Space scientists also look on the moon as special. Its size and distance mean that they can reach it with a rocket fairly easily, and this means that they can practice "at home" before reaching out for the planets. In time, explorers may well use the moon as a take-off point for journeys beyond. The reason is that the moon's gravity is considerably lower than the earth's. For example, a spaceship would have to attain a speed of 26,000 miles an hour to escape the earth and coast to Venus. Escaping from the moon on a trip to Venus, the same ship would require a speed of only 7,000 miles an hour.

For those reasons, man's first destination in space will be the moon.

On arrival explorers are likely to find a small, dead, airless world.

Some astronomers say that the moon is completely airless. Others think it may have a very thin atmosphere, between 1/10,000 and 1/1,000,000 as dense as ours. From our point of view, such a thin atmosphere would be little better than none. We could not breathe it. We could not live in it without pressurized spacesuits. It would not protect us from meteorites or the sun's radiation. It would not carry sound.

The moon also lacks surface water. On it we shall find no oceans, no lakes, no streams. If the moon ever had water, it has long since disappeared. Without an atmosphere, water would turn to vapor. It

34

would float away into space, since the moon's gravity is much too weak to hold such vapor captive.

With no atmosphere and no water, the moon has no weather. Clouds never fill its sky. Rain and snow never moisten its surface. But the moon does have a climate, a terrible one of extreme heat and extreme cold.

The moon's day is about 28 earth days long—the time the moon takes to spin once on its axis. So periods of daylight and darkness each last two weeks. One side of the moon bakes in the sun for 14 days while the other freezes in darkness. The heat is very hot and the cold is very cold because there is no atmosphere to moderate them.

The same lack of atmosphere makes it hard to measure temperatures on the moon. On the earth,

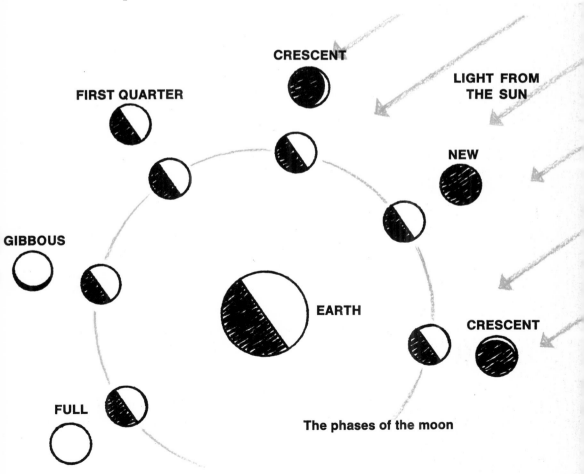

The phases of the moon

we measure the temperature of the air. On the moon, only the surface temperatures of solid objects can be measured. These vary greatly, depending on the color of the object, the material it's made of, and the angle at which sunlight hits it.

A flat, dark rock in full sunlight is much hotter than a light-colored rock; the dark color absorbs sunlight, while the light tends to reflect it. The side of a cliff is cooler than either because it receives only slanting sunlight. So the moon's surface has no one temperature by day. However, rocks exposed to direct sunlight reach temperatures higher than 250 degrees Fahrenheit.

Once the sun sets, the darkened surface of the moon cools quickly. Temperatures drop far below zero. By the end of the two-week night they may be as low as minus 260 degrees, giving the moon a temperature range of at least 510 degrees.

A harsh climate but no air, no water, no weather —these few facts explain much about the moon's appearance.

The moon's landscape is marked by the sharp lines of gaunt mountains, great craters, and deep cracks that have probably looked much the same for millions or billions of years. On this rugged land, unlike the earth, there is no erosion: no rain to wear down rocks, no wind to shape them with driving sand, no frost to pry off slivers. There is no vegetation to hide old scars. The moon's landscape is shaped chiefly by the impact of meteorites and the great range of temperature, which causes rock to expand and contract and may wrench apart great rock formations.

Mapping the face of the moon, astronomers have

36

found ten lofty mountain ranges and many single peaks reaching thousands of feet above the surface. They have also noted some thirty plains. Dark gray in color and shaped like rough circles, the plains are the largest features we see on the moon. Together they cover almost half of the moon's visible surface. To early astronomers, the dark plains looked like bodies of water. That is why the plains were given names such as Mare Nubium (Sea of Clouds), Oceanus Procellarum (Ocean of Storms), and Sinus Medii (Central Bay).

Then there are several hundred great clefts, called rills, in the surface of the moon. Through a telescope they look like crooked cracks, many of them about half a mile wide and 90 miles long. No one knows how deep they are or what lies at the bottom of them. They may have been caused by moonquakes or some similar movement of rock. Volcanoes may also have played a part in forming them. Photographs from a moon probe showed mountainous heaps of volcanic material along the edge of one rill.

The most eye-catching features of the moon are its ring-shaped craters. Giant ones are between 60 and 150 miles in diameter—far bigger than any craters known on Earth. Astronomers have counted more than 30,000 craters, ranging in diameter from 10 to 150 miles. In addition, the moon's surface is pockmarked with tiny craters too numerous to count.

The giant craters are ringed by mountains, some of which rise 17,000 feet from the surface of the moon. On the outside of a crater the mountain slopes are gentle. On the inside, they drop off sharply to the sunken floor of the crater. The floor may be

The rays surrounding the crater Tycho

A closer view of Tycho

several thousand feet below the level of the plains. In some craters the floor appears to be smooth. In others mountain peaks rise from the floor.

Reaching out from some of the craters are brilliant streaks, called rays. Some, like those of the crater Tycho, extend for hundreds of miles. Astronomers are not sure what the rays are. The rays may be veins of rock or they may be dust-fine material blown from the craters when these were formed.

Scientists think that the craters probably formed in three different ways. Some may be the result of fractures in the moon's crust. Some may have been formed by volcanic action; perhaps when the moon was young, rings of mountains forced their way up and molten lava flowed out of cracks, forming the floors of the craters. Most of the craters were probably formed when meteorites struck the moon.

Millions or billions of years ago when the moon and Earth were young, the solar system was full of wandering chunks of rocks, or **meteoroids**. The rocks, some of which were the size of mountains, bombarded both the moon and the earth.

Meteorites travel at tremendous speeds: some that hit the earth are traveling at 30 miles a second, which is 108,000 miles an hour. Such speed gives them energy equal to 250 times their own weight in dynamite. When a meteorite hits, it is brought to a sudden stop. The stop releases the meteorite's energy largely in the form of heat.

That, scientists think, is what happened on the moon. Mountain-sized rocks whipping through space slammed into the moon. Their energy was released as heat so great that it turned the meteorite and the

38

surrounding rock into gas. The temperature of the gas reached several million degrees which means that it had enormous pressure. Like an exploding bomb, it expanded and (silently) blew a giant crater.

On the earth we see only a few signs of these ancient explosions. Scientists think that most crater scars have been smoothed by erosion or hidden by plant life. They also think that after a time the bombardment of the earth stopped. Most of the giant meteoroids were gone. And only a large meteoroid can penetrate the earth's atmosphere. Smaller ones burn up before they reach the earth's surface, because of friction with the earth's atmosphere.

The moon is different. Without an atmosphere, it has been struck by meteorites of all sizes. Craters lie within craters. Craters overlap craters, forming a lacy pattern. On the moon's airless surface, no erosion takes place and no plants grow. So the craters remain, scars of violent explosions.

The curious thing about the craters is that there are more of them on the side of the moon that faces the earth than on the far side. This is one of several discoveries of the space age, for until recent years no human being had ever seen the far side of the moon.

Long ago, the moon's rotation slowed down to 27⅓ earth days, which is also the time required for the moon to complete one orbit of the earth. For this reason, the moon always shows us the same face.

Now United States and Soviet rockets have passed behind the moon and photographed the far side. The photos show the same kinds of mountains, plains, and craters that mark the moon's face, but the far side seems to be much smoother.

39

Television picture of the moon's surface transmitted by Ranger IV, *about 1,470 miles above the surface*

Some scientists think that the near side of the moon has been more heavily bombarded by meteorites. Other scientists suggest a different explanation. They think that the tug of Earth's gravity has affected the near side of the moon. Some surface markings may have been caused by the stresses and strains of this pull.

Another space-age discovery is that the moon, unlike the earth, has no magnetic field. This probably means that it is cold and solid at its center.

No one knows for sure what is at the center of the earth. But most scientists think that the earth has hot molten iron or iron and nickel at its center. They think that movement in the molten iron is responsible for the earth's magnetic field. That is, it makes the earth act like a giant magnet. A magnetic field surrounds the earth in space and traps certain kinds of radiation. As a result, the earth is surrounded by a giant belt of radiation.

The moon, lacking a magnetic field, has no radiation belt. This means that the moon's surface is bombarded by many kinds of radiation that never reach the earth. This radiation is one of the dangers from which explorers of the moon must be protected.

For many years scientists wondered if the very surface of the moon might also be a danger. Some thought that the moon might be covered with thick layers of very fine dust thrown out by exploding meteorites. In places, they guessed, the dust might be thousands of feet deep, and for the unwary explorer who blundered into it, the dust would be more treacherous than quicksand. Other scientists thought that the plains and perhaps the crater bottoms might have

40

been formed by molten lava. If so, the ground underneath the lava might prove too porous and full of cavities to support a spaceship or even the weight of a man.

Now that spacecraft have landed on various parts of the moon, space scientists are much encouraged. The craft did not break through the crust. Nor were they swallowed up in dust. This means that at least some parts of the moon are safe to land on.

Photographs from the moon show a somewhat gritty-looking surface that appears to be strewn with

41

pebbles and boulders. Parts of it look rather like a freshly plowed field. Spacecraft that have hopped on the surface have left footprints. Both American and Soviet scientists think that hard material lies a short distance below the powdery surface.

Surveyor 3, a U.S. craft, sampled a small patch of the moon's surface. On radio command, its mechanical arm pounded, pressed, and scraped the surface. It banged on rocks. It scooped up a handful of soil and dropped it near the camera's eye. The tests showed that the moon's surface was like sandy soil on the earth.

Surveyor 5 made a chemical analysis of the moon's soil. In the spot studied, the materials proved to be very much like those on the earth. The minerals contained oxygen and silicon, as earth rocks do, and may well have been basalt. (On the earth basalt is produced by volcanoes.) The results of a Soviet probe, Luna 10, also indicate that the moon's plains are formed of basalt.

Does this mean that volcanoes helped to form the moon? That is one of the many, many questions to be answered. The list of things that scientists want to know about the moon is long indeed.

Does the moon have any atmosphere at all? If so, where do the gases come from?

What are the rays? What are the rills? How did the craters form and when did they form?

Are the moon's minerals the same as ours? Or has radiation from the sun and other sources created minerals unknown here?

The answers to such questions will tell us much about the moon, and they will also tell us something

42

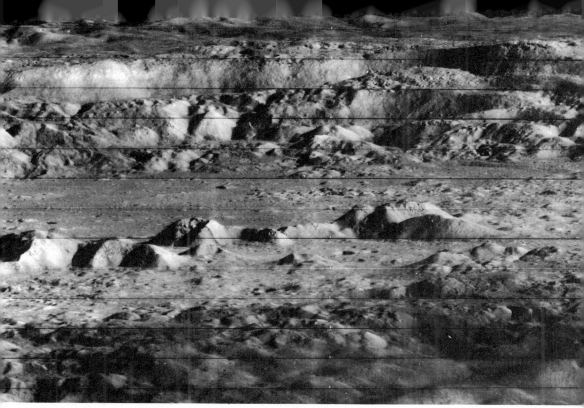

Inside the crater Copernicus. The mountains in the fore-ground are 1,000 feet high.

about the history of the solar system and our own planet. Much of the earth's history has been erased or hidden, sometimes by slow processes such as erosion or the laying down of sediment, sometimes by violent events such as earthquakes or the thrusting up of mountains. The moon remains much as it was at the time it formed, and its history is still written on its face.

What is found on the moon may even tell us where the moon came from in the first place. Did it form from material left over from the earth? Was it torn out of the newly formed earth? Was it perhaps a small planet that the earth captured?

Has life ever existed on the moon? Some scientists think that it may have. Long, long ago, they say, the moon may have had an atmosphere and water. Very simple forms of life may have developed on the moon.

43

A few scientists think there is a chance that some form of life, such as bacteria, might be surviving in cracks and clefts on the moon today. Most scientists do not think that possible. Nor do they think that there was ever life on the moon. But explorers will look for fossils, which would be signs of life in the past, and for tiny primitive forms of life that just might exist on the moon today.

They will also be busy exploring the moon's mineral resources. These resources will determine the uses that man can make of the moon.

Any permanent base will have to be largely self-supporting, for it is impossible to send to the moon everything that men might need. A base will require sources of water, oxygen, food, and fuel. Explorers must find out whether these exist in the moon's minerals.

On the earth a large amount of oxygen is locked in the rocks that form our planet's crust. There is now reason to think that this is true of the moon's rocks too. Water also is locked in the earth's crust. This may be true of the moon. Given enough power, men should be able to release and use the oxygen and water. For power they could convert the energy of sunlight into electricity.

44

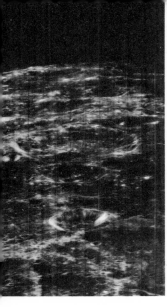

The earth hangs above the moon's horizon.

Given water and oxygen, men could produce food. Plants, for example, can be grown without soil in water. One day it might even be possible to extract from the moon's rocks the chemical elements that form organic molecules. Special food factories could then turn these elements into fats, sugars, starches, and proteins.

If a moon base proves practicable, it will become a taking-off point for space trips. It will also become an observatory for studies of the moon and for astronomy. The moon's lack of atmosphere makes it ideal for astronomical observations.

On the earth the atmosphere tends to shut off radio waves from space. The waves that do penetrate the atmosphere hint of awesome events taking place in our own galaxy and beyond. But they do no more than hint. On the moon, radio telescopes will pick up a much wider range of much stronger radio signals.

The earth's atmosphere also blurs our view of space. Looking through the atmosphere with a powerful telescope is like studying a distant street scene through a window whose glass is wavy and slightly dirty. From the moon, the view through a telescope will be sharp and clear.

To all explorers, astronomers or not, many strange

45

and wondrous things will be visible in the moon's sky.

The moon is a world without dawn or dusk or blue sky, for there is no atmosphere to scatter the sun's light. Just before day the black sky is still full of very bright stars. Then the sun begins to rise. Its faintly glowing **corona,** or halo, appears above the horizon, followed by great arching flames of gas. Finally the sun's disk appears, climbing very, very slowly. It is colder looking and bluer than the sun as we see it from the earth.

Sun, flames and corona move across the sky—and the sky is black. Look away from the sun and you will see the stars. Without the dimming effect of an atmosphere, they are very bright.

Perhaps the most spectacular sight to be seen from the moon is the earth. Hanging in the moon's sky, it goes through phases from crescent to full and back to crescent. It is four times bigger in the moon's sky than the moon is in ours, and it shines with a brighter light.

Look away from the sky, and there is the moon's wild landscape etched in black and white, harsh and grim. Airless, waterless and bathed in dangerous radiation, it is a hostile world for man. Yet it is probably much less hostile than its first cousin Mercury, smallest of the planets.

5

Mercury and Venus

Between the earth and the sun are two planets, Mercury and Venus. Since they are neighbors, you might expect them to be somewhat alike. Yet one is an airless rocky ball, while the other is wrapped in clouds so thick that no one has ever seen through them to the planet's surface.

Mercury is the rocky ball. Scarcely bigger than our moon, it is the smallest planet in the solar system. As the innermost planet, it is also the fastest moving. That is why it is named after fleet-footed Mercury, the messenger of the gods. Traveling the long ellipse of its orbit, Mercury takes only 88 earth days to complete one trip around the sun. That is, a year on Mercury is 88 earth days long.

Strange as it may seem, a day on Mercury—the time from one sunrise to the next—is about twice as long as a year. One day on Mercury is about 180 earth days long.

The length of Mercury's day is a recent discovery made by radar and radio astronomers. It came as a surprise to everyone.

47

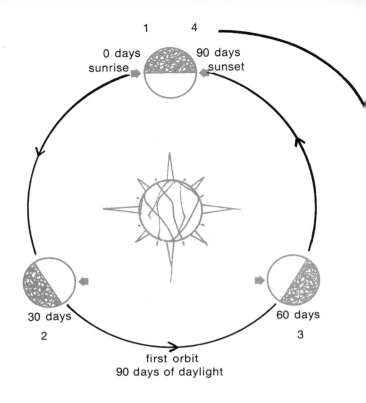

first orbit
90 days of daylight

Astronomers had long thought that Mercury took the same time to rotate that it did to orbit the sun: 88 earth days. This meant that Mercury always kept the same face toward the sun, just as the moon always keeps the same face toward the earth. The side of Mercury facing the sun was a land of ever-day, continuously exposed to blazing heat. The temperature of the surface had to be more than 700 degrees Fahrenheit, so hot that lead and tin would melt. The night side never saw the sun. Its only light came from the stars and planets. Its only heat, if there was any, was a trickle reaching it through the ground. The temperature there had to be minus 450 degrees, only a little above absolute zero.

Recently, however, radio astronomers began to question this picture of Mercury. With radio telescopes they had been picking up radio waves from Mercury, and radio waves from a heated body give an indication of its temperature. The radio waves from Mercury seemed to show that the dark side was

48

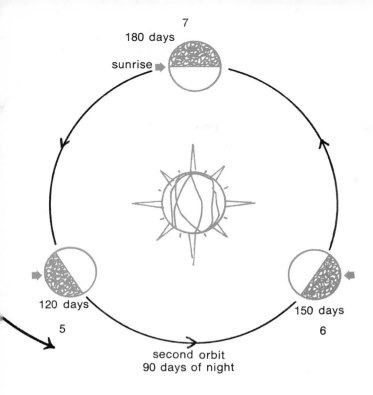

7
180 days

sunrise ➡

120 days

5

150 days

6

second orbit
90 days of night

much warmer than anyone had thought. This suggested that the planet might not always keep the same face toward the sun, that its period of rotation was not 88 days.

Astronomers began to probe Mercury with radar and to analyze the echoes. The echoes indicated that Mercury was rotating every 58 to 59 earth days. Checking these findings against new mathematical calculations, astronomers concluded that Mercury rotates once every $58\frac{1}{2}$ earth days.

Mercury, then takes $58\frac{1}{2}$ earth days to spin once on its axis and 88 earth days to orbit the sun. As a result, its solar day (one period of daylight and darkness) is about 180 earth days long. This fact surprises most people, but the diagram will help you to understand why it is so.

This new finding means that Mercury does not have a side of ever-day and a side of ever-night. Rather, a given point on the planet travels through dark and light every 180 earth days. It is both cooled

49

MERCURY

average diameter	2,900 miles
average distance from sun	35,960,000 miles
average speed of revolution	107,900 miles per hour
length of year	88 earth days
length of solar day	180 earth days
period of rotation	58½ earth days
gravity	0.26 of Earth's
temperature on night side	$-9.6°$ F.
transits	1970, 1973, 1986, 1993, 1999
moons	none

Mercury, disappearing behind the edge of the solar disk

and heated. Radio astronomers now think that the subsurface temperature during Mercury's night is about minus 9.6 degrees.

The results of the new studies make Mercury seem a little more inviting than it once did. But it is still a forbidding place for man. The planet must be a parched globe where sunlight blazes on the daylight side and everything looks white in the intense glare. The landscape must be as rugged and bleak as the moon's. There must be huge craters formed by meteorites, gaunt mountains, and gigantic fissures, cracked open by extremes of temperature.

But to describe Mercury is to guess, for no one has ever had a really good look at the innermost planet. Astronomers studying its surface can make out only

50

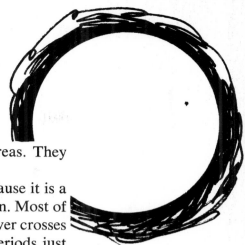

what appear to be light areas and dark areas. They see no details.

Mercury is difficult to see and study because it is a small planet that lies between us and the sun. Most of the time it is hidden by the sun's glare. It never crosses our night sky but appears only for short periods just after sunset and just before sunrise. In effect, it sets and rises with the sun. The planet can be seen only if the sky is very clear.

Mercury, as it transits across the sun, appears as no more than a black dot.

A telescope shows that Mercury goes through phases. The phases occur because Mercury lies inside the earth's orbit and so we see the planet lighted at various angles. The phases are like the moon's except for one thing. We never see a full Mercury. When the full face is turned toward the earth, the sun's glare hides the planet from view.

From time to time we also see Mercury crossing the sun. Every few years Mercury appears to edge onto the left side of the sun's disk, taking shape as a small black dot. If the planet blocked more of the sun from view, this would be counted an **eclipse**. As it is, Mercury's crossing of the sun is called a **transit**.

Transits long provided astronomers with one of their few clues to what Mercury must be like. They reasoned that if Mercury had as much atmosphere as the earth, it would shine as a halo each time that the planet was in transit. Since no halo could be seen, astronomers knew that Mercury must have little or no atmosphere.

New studies with a spectroscope confirm this. They show that Mercury has just a trace of an atmosphere. Carbon dioxide is the only gas that has been detected in it.

51

Astronomers think that Mercury probably once had an atmosphere and lost it. Orbiting the sun at an average distance of 36 million miles, the planet was subjected to intense heat. The heat speeded up the movement of the gas molecules in the atmosphere. And Mercury's gravity, which is about one third as strong as the earth's, was too weak to hold the envelope of air. Most of the gases escaped into space, leaving only a trace of the heaviest.

Mercury became what it is today—a bare and barren ball of rock baking in the rays of a blazing sun.

Venus is one of the loveliest planets, and it has long been one of the most tantalizing. It comes closer to us than any other planet, sometimes swinging within 26 million miles of the earth. It is at times brighter than any other planet or star in our sky. And in several ways it appears to be an Earthlike planet. It lies in the same belt of space as the earth, and its diameter, mass and gravity are all just a little less than ours. But we cannot see the planet's surface. Venus is cloaked in dense, gleaming clouds that are a faint lemon-yellow in color.

The clouds make Venus so bright that you can see it in broad daylight if you know where and when to look. The same brightness has made it one of the most familiar planets even though, like Mercury, it appears in the night sky for only short periods after sunset and before sunrise.

To the ancients, who named lovely Venus after the goddess of love, such behavior was puzzling. It was not really understood until the time of Galileo.

52

Then astronomers finally learned that the planets circled the sun and that the orbit of Venus lay between the earth and sun.

With the invention of the telescope, many astronomers began to study Venus closely. They assumed that what they saw was the surface of the planet and they began to make drawings of it. Around 1730 an Italian astronomer produced a map showing oceans, continents, and other features that resembled the earth's. A number of other astronomers also reported surface markings on Venus.

Today there is every reason to believe that those astronomers were mistaken. It is most unlikely that anyone ever saw the planet's surface. Earlier astronomers were most likely seeing the markings that appear in Venus' atmosphere.

Modern telescopes show light and dark patches that appear and disappear. They may last for a few days or they may vanish in a matter of hours. Probably they are caused by the thickening or thinning of clouds torn by raging winds below.

Certain other strange markings also appear on Venus from time to time. When Venus is in its crescent phase, two bright patches are often seen at the tips of the horns. No one knows what these are.

Then at times a strange pale light shines on the dark (or night) side of Venus. Astronomers call it ashen light, but they are not sure of what it is. Some think it may be earthshine—a reflection of light from the earth. Others think it may be akin to the auroras seen in the earth's sky. Earthly auroras are caused by electrified particles that make the atmosphere glow.

53

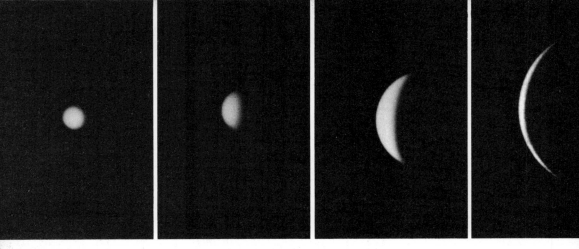

Five phases of Venus as seen through a telescope

It is quite possible that something similar takes place in the atmosphere of Venus.

For many years, observations of the atmosphere gave astronomers their chief clues to conditions of Venus. The shape of the atmosphere, for example, indicated that Venus must be a slowly rotating planet. If it were rotating as fast as the earth, its atmosphere would have the shape of a slightly flattened ball. Since there was no flattening, Venus could not be rotating nearly as fast as the earth.

Studies with a spectroscope showed that Venus' atmosphere contained large amounts of carbon dioxide. Scientists thought there might be other gases in the atmosphere, too, but in such small quantities that they did not show up in the spectroscope.

With a carbon-dioxide atmosphere, Venus was likely to be a very hot planet. Heat from the sun would penetrate the atmosphere in short-wave radiation. The planet's surface would absorb the heat and give it off in long waves. Most of the long waves would be blocked by the carbon dioxide and trapped on Venus. So, scientists reasoned, Venus must be rather like a greenhouse, where short waves pass through the glass and long waves are trapped inside.

There matters stood until a few years ago. Then radio and radar studies were made of Venus, and spacecraft began to probe the planet. The results

54

VENUS

average diameter	7,600 miles
average distance from sun	67,200,000 miles
average speed of revolution	79,000 miles an hour
length of year	225 earth days
length of solar day	115 earth days
period of rotation	243 earth days
gravity	0.85 of Earth's
surface temperature	uncertain: 500° to 800°F.
transits	1874, 1882, 2004, 2012
moons	none

confirmed the earlier observations and also produced a number of surprises. Venus, which astronomers had thought of as the earth's "cloudy twin," now appears to be startlingly different from our own planet.

In the early 1960's radar was turned on Venus. Analysis of the radar echoes produced the first surprises.

One was that Venus rotates backward: from east to west. On Venus the sun must rise in the west and set in the east.

55

A second was that Venus takes 243 earth days to spin once. This figure confirmed that Venus is indeed a slowly rotating planet, but it also meant that Venus is a very odd planet. It not only spins from east to west but also takes longer to spin once than to orbit the sun. Venus orbits the sun once every 225 earth days.

Something else is even stranger. Venus always turns the same face toward the earth as it overtakes our planet. In some way the earth's gravity seems to affect Venus' rate of spinning.

As computers analyzed radar echoes from Venus, scientists received the first clues to what that planet's surface is like The echoes indicated two large, rough areas on Venus. One runs 2,400 miles north and south and is several hundred miles wide. The other runs east and west and is even more extensive. At present no one knows what these surface features are, because radar tell nothing of height. The features may be small bumps, such as fields of boulders. Or they may be towering mountain ranges comparable to the Rockies.

The surface of Venus may be extremely windy. Ultraviolet photographs of the clouds indicate that they rotate every four to five days. That is 50 times faster than the solid body of the planet is rotating. If there is really such a great difference in the rates of rotation, then the surface is being swept by steady winds of more than 100 miles an hour.

The surface is also very hot. A three-year study of Venus by radio telescope gave an average surface temperature of 585 degrees. In 1962 the United

56

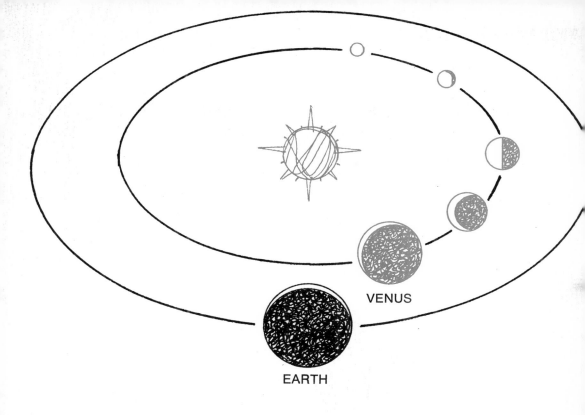

States space probe Mariner 2 passed close to Venus and sent back temperature readings of 800 degrees. (This is the heat level used in self-cleaning kitchen ovens. It turns boiled-over remains of food into fine dust.) Many scientists thought Mariner's figures too high. They suggested that the instruments had measured not the surface temperature but something else, such as heat radiation from lightning flashes. Then in 1967 the Soviet spacecraft Venus 4 soft-landed an instrumented capsule on Venus. It reported a surface temperature of 536 degrees. That is about the heat level used for broiling meat, and it poses many problems for manned exploration of Venus. It also poses problems for unmanned exploration, since few of today's electronic devices could function at temperatures of more than 500 degrees.

Buoyed by a parachute, the Soviet capsule made a

The phases of Venus seen from the earth

57

 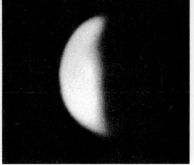 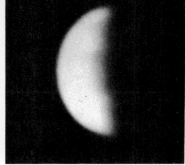

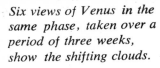

Six views of Venus in the same phase, taken over a period of three weeks, show the shifting clouds.

90-minute float-down through 16 miles of Venus' atmosphere. It analyzed the gases of the atmosphere and measured atmospheric pressures as well as temperatures. Shortly after the float-down, the United States spacecraft Mariner 5 made a two-hour fly-by of Venus. It carried instruments to analyze the atmosphere and to search for radiation belts and magnetic fields.

Both probes found that the atmosphere of Venus is much more dense than the earth's. At the planet's surface the atmosphere may be 15 to 22 times as dense as ours at sea level. As a result, one Mariner scientist said, Venus might be a planet of weird optical illusions. At such densities, light is trapped and bent so sharply that an explorer would have good reason not to believe his eyes. The horizon would always appear high, giving a person the impression that he was standing at the bottom of a bowl. A vehicle traveling away from the explorer would appear to be rising in the sky, rather than vanishing over the horizon. At night the sun would seem to be setting on one horizon and, at the same time, rising on the other.

One other thing would also be strange about night on Venus. As darkness falls, the night side has a faint ultraviolet glow. Mariner scientists think this may be caused by electrical discharges or chemical reactions in the upper atmosphere.

Mariner 5 found no trace of a radiation belt like the one that girdles the earth. Neither probe found signs of a magnetic field. This was a great disappointment. Measurements of a magnetic field would have

58

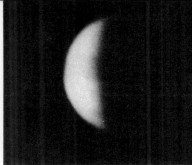

provided clues to both the interior and the surface of Venus.

Both probes confirmed that the atmosphere of Venus is made up chiefly of carbon dioxide. The Soviet probe found some water vapor and free oxygen. The United States probe found traces of hydrogen but no free oxygen.

Venus' carbon-dioxide atmosphere is one of the great puzzles facing scientists. They think that long ago the young earth had an atmosphere that was rich in carbon dioxide. As time passed, much of the carbon dioxide combined with substances in the earth's crust, forming rock such as limestone.

Why, scientists wonder, didn't the same thing happen on Venus? Is Venus evolving more slowly than the earth? Or has Venus already evolved but in a totally different way? Is it possible that Venus and the earth were not born at the same time and in the same way?

Those are just a few of the questions that scientists have to answer. They wonder, too, why there is little or no nitrogen in Venus' atmosphere, when nitrogen makes up 80 percent of the earth's. They still do not know what the clouds are made of or what the planet's surface is like. They wonder why Venus is as hot as it is and how air circulates around the planet.

They wonder, too, about the possibility of life on Venus. The planet's heat would rule out most forms of life that we know. Yet there may be cooler regions on Venus, near the poles or, if there are mountains, at the mountaintops. There may even be polar icecaps with small oceans or fresh-water lakes at their

59

edges. So some Soviet and American scientists still think that simple forms of life, such as microbes, may exist on Venus.

In the years to come, much more will be learned about Venus as the planet is probed with radar and rockets. Someday in the future valiant explorers may even descend through the clouds.

But that day will not come for a long time. The first planet men will visit is almost certain to be our other close neighbor, Mars.

6

Mars, the Red Planet

In a number of ways, Mars is much like the earth. It is a small, solid planet, whose diameter is a little more than half of the earth's. Among the inner planets, only Mars and Earth have moons. Mars has two tiny ones. Since its axis is tilted like ours, Mars has seasons—spring, summer, fall, and winter. Being farther from the sun, Mars travels a longer orbit at speeds slower than the earth's. As a result, its year is almost twice as long as ours; its seasons are longer; and its climate is colder. But a day on Mars is only 41 minutes longer than a day on Earth.

Finally, there are signs that life may exist on Mars. That is what makes Mars the most exciting planet. It also makes Mars the most controversial. For nearly a century, scientists have been arguing over the question of life on Mars.

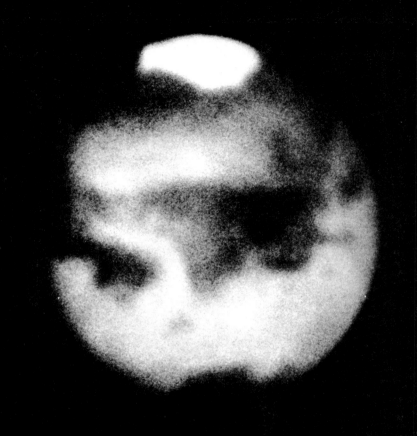

MARS

average diameter	4,200 miles
average distance from sun	141,600,000 miles
average speed of revolution	54,200 miles per hour
length of year	687 earth days
length of day	24½ earth hours
gravity	0.38 of Earth's
temperature at equator in summer	
by day	70° F.
by night	−110° F. ?
moons	2

If you could look at Mars through a big telescope, you would find it rather disappointing. You would see only a rather fuzzy, reddish ball marked with vague dark patches. Depending on when you looked at Mars, you might also see a white patch at the pole tilted toward you. But you would see nothing that was likely to stir up an argument, for you would see no details. It takes the practiced eye of an astronomer to see Mars fairly clearly.

Viewed without a telescope in the night sky, Mars has a reddish hue. In ancient times, this color won Mars its name. The color reminded people of blood, and so the planet was named for the god of war.

The telescope shows that Mars looks red because it is red. Most of its surface is covered with reddish regions that range in tone from deep red to yellowish white.

The red regions never change from season to season or year to year. But from time to time a yellow veil spreads over them, in the way that sandstorms sweep certain parts of the earth. For these reasons, astronomers think that the red regions must be sandy deserts. Their color may come from rusting iron oxide, like the red in Arizona's Painted Desert.

The brilliant white icecaps stand out more clearly than any other feature of Mars, and they are very interesting. Here there is movement and change. In regular rhythm the icecaps advance and retreat with the seasons.

By winter's end an icecap may cover some four million square miles. With the coming of spring, it begins to shrink. It changes at first slowly, then with increasing speed. By mid-spring, dark cracks appear

63

  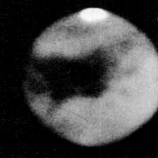

The spread of Mars' southern polar cap and the lightening of its dark patches. (South is at the top because the image is inverted in the telescope.)

in the cap. The ice splits into big sections; the big sections split into small ones.

Near the end of summer, patches of white cloud appear in the polar region. By fall they have curtained the entire area. When the veil of clouds breaks up in late winter, the icecap has re-formed.

In some years, the icecaps are bigger than in other years. But the general pattern is always the same. Even the dark cracks appear in the same places every year. Probably the ice is running into obstacles, such as hills or low mountains, and tearing apart.

The Martian icecaps are not thick fields of ice and snow, like the earth's. They seem to be just a thin covering of frost, perhaps an inch thick.

These thin caps of ice are the only water known to exist on Mars. Melt them and they might just about fill Lake Erie. In a way, that doesn't seem like enough water to make much difference. Yet when the icecaps start to melt, a second very interesting change occurs. This change takes place in the dark patches that cover a fifth of Mars' surface.

Astronomers cannot be sure what the dark patches are. But they watch with fascination the changes that come over them. When a polar icecap melts, a wave of color washes over the dark areas in that hemisphere. Along with the color change come changes in shape and size.

The changes begin near the edge of the melting polar cap and move toward the equator. It is almost certain that the changes are caused by the melting. But no one knows whether the melting ice runs to-

64

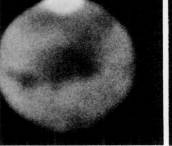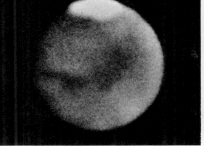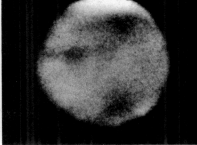

ward the equator as surface water. Possibly it moves above the surface, traveling to the other pole in the form of water vapor.

What are the dark patches? Are they regions of plant life that waken under the magic touch of water? Or are they something else?

Modern scientific arguments about life on Mars hinge on those questions. But the argument itself goes back more than eighty years to the famous study of Mars made by Giovanni Schiaparelli, an Italian astronomer.

Schiaparelli's study began in 1877. That year Mars was in an excellent position for observation. It was close to the earth and fully lighted by the sun. Schiaparelli himself was a fine astronomer with a very good telescope. Everything, then, was just right. It resulted in the first detailed description of Mars and the start of a great argument.

Like other astronomers of his time, Schiaparelli thought that the dark areas were seas and the reddish areas continents. But he found a great range of colors in both. He noted certain areas that were sometimes yellow and sometimes brown or black like the "seas." These, he thought, must be swamps.

Searching out more and more detail, Schiaparelli noted a number of dark streaks on the face of Mars. They appeared to be thin dark lines that crossed the "continents" and linked the "seas." Schiaparelli called the lines *canali*, which is the Italian word for "channels."

The longer he studied Mars, the more *canali* he

65

found. Mapping them, he discovered they formed a network, lacing the planet and crisscrossing one another. And in many ways they were rather curious:

(1) The lines ran straight and true. They did not look at all like the rivers of Earth, which curve and meander and sometimes twist back on themselves. However, they did always seem to link the dark areas. And where they crossed one another there was usually a small dark patch. Schiaparelli thought these dark spots were lakes.

(2) The lines varied greatly in size. Some *canali* were short and narrow, perhaps 200 miles long and 50 miles wide. Some ran straight across Mars for a thousand miles or more and were 100 to 200 miles wide. Short or long, each had a definite beginning and a definite end.

(3) Sometimes *canali* disappeared. The change might take place in a week or it might take a year. But it always happened in the same way. The color of a line would grow gradually lighter until it blended with the surrounding land and the line vanished. The reverse also happened. *Canali* might suddenly appear where none had been before. Schiaparelli explained the changes this way. The *canali,* he said, are deep furrows in the land. In spring and summer polar ice melts and water flows into the furrows. This gives them their dark color. Then, as the water soaks into the ground and also evaporates, the furrows dry up and vanish.

(4) Certain *canali* doubled. This change usually took place in the months just before or after the melting of a polar icecap. *Canali* that had been single lines would double in the course of a few days or a few hours. Where there had been just one line, a

66

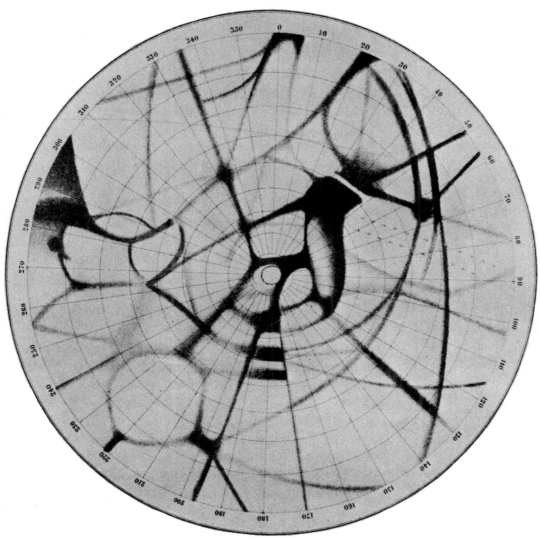

Schiaparelli's drawing of the northern hemisphere of Mars

second would appear. It was parallel to the first, running beside it so that the two looked like railroad tracks. The distance between the two lines might range from 30 miles to 400 miles.

Schiaparelli was not the first man to see dark lines on Mars. But nobody else had studied them so long and carefully. Nobody else had found so many. Nobody else had mapped them. And nobody else had given them a name. Schiaparelli's name for the lines

67

meant "channels." But as his work was translated into English people did not use that word. Instead they used "canals," perhaps because that English word was so like the Italian *canali*.

The change was an important one. A channel can be a natural waterway or it can be man-made. A canal is always man-made. The very use of the word "canals" implied that intelligent beings had built them.

Then there was the nature of the *canali*. They ran absolutely straight and true. They appeared to be part of a plan. Surely, people said, the *canali* could not have occurred naturally. They must have been built—and for a purpose. If this was so, then intelligent life must exist on Mars or must have existed there in the past.

The *canali* touched off a storm of argument about life on Mars. Some people said they were proof of life on Mars. Others claimed life on Mars was impossible. Schiaparelli himself never took a stand on this matter. He did not think the *canali* were proof of life; neither did he think life on Mars was impossible.

The argument became even more heated as other astronomers turned their telescopes on Mars. Some claimed to have seen just what Schiaparelli did. Some failed to see any *canali* at all. And that raised the question of whether the *canali* really existed.

Among the astronomers who reported seeing *canali* was an American, Percival Lowell. Like Schiaparelli, Lowell had made Mars his special study. In 1894 he set up an observatory at Flagstaff, Arizona, to study the planets, particularly Mars.

One of the first discoveries made by Lowell con-

68

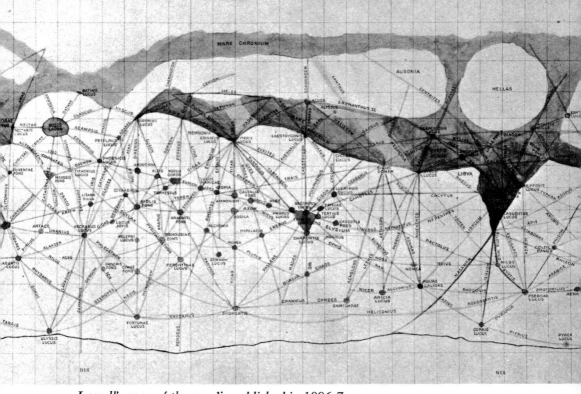

Lowell's map of the canali, *published in 1896-7*

cerned the dark areas or "seas." Working in the clear, dry air of Arizona, he observed the "seas" in far greater detail than anyone before him. And what he saw convinced him that they could not be large bodies of water.

For one thing, the dark areas, like the reddish ones, were crossed by *canali*. Further, the dark areas changed both their color and their shape from season to season.

Soon after an icecap started to melt, *canali* appeared in the polar regions. The darkening of *canali* spread toward the equator and beyond it at a rate of about 50 miles a day. At the same time, the dark areas changed their shapes. And during the wet season their color changed from a dusky shade to green and later to brown and yellow.

The dark areas might be marshes. But Lowell believed that the change of color was actually much

69

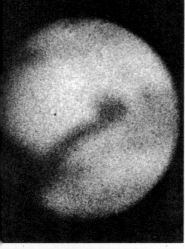

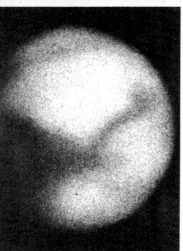

The face of Mars changes as the planet rotates.

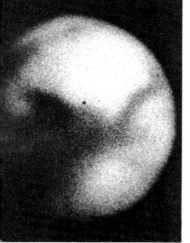

more meaningful. He believed that the dark patches consisted of plant life that responded to the seasons just as our plant life does.

Year after year Lowell studied the *canali,* the dark areas, the changes that took place on the face of Mars. As he did so, an idea began to take shape in his mind, an idea that gave meaning to the *canali* and told a tragic story. This was Lowell's famous theory about Mars, which he announced in 1906. Lowell believed that Mars had once supported a great civilization; then a drastic change turned Mars into a dying planet where life was slowly but surely being snuffed out.

This is the way Lowell reasoned:

If we could stand off in space and look at the earth, every six months we would see a strange and beautiful change taking place. In spring half of the earth would start to waken from its winter's sleep. White and browns would vanish. In their place would come a spreading light green that moved slowly toward the pole and at the same time became darker.

On Mars, Lowell pointed out, something very similar happens. In spring we see a wave of changing color spread across half the planet. But there is one important difference. On the earth, green starts near the equator and moves toward the pole. On Mars the wave of color starts near the pole and moves toward the equator. The reason for the difference is water.

On the earth, water is always available, except in deserts. Plants, then, are called to life by the sun and by the sun alone. But Mars, Lowell said, is different. Its plant life finds no water in the soil and so is doubly

70

dependent on the sun. Mars' plant life needs the warmth of the sun, just as the earth's plants do. But it cannot grow until the sun has melted the icecap and unlocked the water supply. For this reason, Martian plants first show signs of new life near the pole. That is where water first becomes available. As the water spreads toward the equator, plants along the way begin their spring growth.

Next, Lowell took up the question of intelligent life on Mars. It is easy, he pointed out, to see the spread and growth of plants on another planet. By their presence they change the color and shape of whole regions. But we would not see similar signs of animal life. In fact, we would recognize animal life "not by its body, but by its mind," Lowell wrote. "Across the gulf of space it could be recognized only by the imprint it had made on the face of Mars."

The imprint, he said, was the canals—the long straight lines that only intelligent beings might have made. As he had seen and drawn them, the canals were clearly artificial and made for a purpose.

Their purpose, said Lowell, was to carry water across the dry planet and irrigate the fertile regions where the Martians lived.

How could they carry water all over Mars when water runs only downhill? Lowell supposed that the Martians must have built a vast pumping system to move water through the canals. The power required, he calculated, would be 4,000 times the power of Niagara Falls. Such a power system was a great engineering achievement. It could have been built only by beings who were intelligent—and desperate.

71

The Martians, according to Lowell, had good reason to be desperate. They had to build canals and pumping stations because the water supply was failing. Slowly, over a long period of time, Mars had become drier and drier. To supply their needs, the Martians reached out to what sources of water remained. They built canals and pumped water to places where it was needed, much as we pipe water to big cities. As the planet grew still drier, its surface was laced with canals. Finally the Martians had to tap their one last source of water: the distant icecaps. Their very lives depended on the yearly melting of the icecaps. For this reason their whole way of life centered around the canals and pumping stations.

At best, Lowell said, the Martians were simply buying time. There was no way in which they could halt the drying up of their planet, no way in which they could preserve their scanty supply of water. One day the water would be gone.

At the end of his book, *Mars as the Abode of Life,* Lowell said of Mars: "The process that brought it to its present pass must go on to the bitter end, until the last spark of Martian life goes out. The drying up of the planet is certain to proceed until its surface can support no life at all. Slowly but surely time will snuff it out. When the last ember is thus extinguished, the planet will roll, a dead world, through space."

That, very briefly, is Lowell's account of life on Mars. As everyone agrees, it is a brilliant theory. But if you ask how close it comes to fact—that's where the argument begins.

If Mars is really laced with canals, then Lowell's theory may well be true. But if there are no canals,

72

MARS AT
OPPOSITION

EARTH

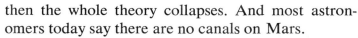

then the whole theory collapses. And most astronomers today say there are no canals on Mars.

If there are no *canali,* then what did Schiaparelli and Lowell see? Or, if there are *canali,* why don't today's astronomers see them? In fact, why don't all astronomers see the same thing when they look at Mars?

The answers to those questions lie in the problems of viewing Mars and recording what one has seen. For, while astronomers see Mars better than any other planet, their view of it is still far from ideal.

To begin with, any time we look out from Earth into the solar system, our view is blurred. We cannot see clearly through the earth's atmosphere. There is no way to bring Mars into strong, sharp focus.

Secondly, astronomers cannot observe Mars night after night and always get the same view, as they do with the moon. The distance between Earth and Mars varies greatly. For one thing, the shapes of their orbits are different. Mars orbits the sun in an ellipse. Earth's orbit is almost a circle. And, of course, the two planets move at different speeds. As a result, Earth passes Mars only once every twenty-six months.

When Earth does pass Mars, the two planets are said to be in **opposition.** At these times Mars, Earth, and the sun are lined up. Astronomers see the face of Mars fully lighted. Some oppositions are better than others. The two planets may be as much as 62 million miles apart. But once every fifteen years Mars is in opposition and only 35 million miles away.

All of this means that occasionally Mars can be seen much better than at other times.

A third problem has to do with recording what is

73

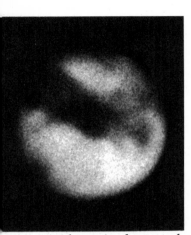

A telescopic photograph of Mars

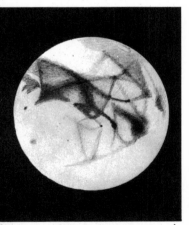

and an astronomer's drawing made at the same time.

seen. We can photograph Mars, but the results are never very clear. Since Mars shines by reflected light, it must be photographed with a time exposure. And movements of the earth's atmosphere blur the picture. The best records of Mars are made by observers who draw what they see. But it is almost impossible to draw in detail everything that the eye has seen at any one moment.

And this raises still a fourth problem: the observer himself. Some people see better than others. Some have more experience in observing through a telescope. Some draw better. To make matters worse, when a detail is faintly glimpsed it may look like one thing to one person and something completely different to another. Finally, our eyes do sometimes trick us. Look down the railroad, and your eyes tell you that the tracks meet in the distance. Turn a photo of the moon upside down, and what looked like a crater may suddenly turn into a mountain.

For all these reasons, observers report having seen Mars in different ways.

A number of astronomers, including some very great ones, claim to have seen *canali* on Mars. Perhaps they really did see them. Perhaps they saw better than other men. Perhaps they were more expert at picking out details. Perhaps Mars has changed—drying up more—since their time.

But most modern scientists say that there is no network of *canali* on Mars. They have seen only a few dark lines on Mars. Photographs show only a few. And these lines, the astronomers say, mark natural formations.

74

The same astronomers make this point, too: our eyes have a tendency to link a series of vague, distant markings and see them as a straight line. You can test this yourself if you draw a row of dots an eighth of an inch apart on a sheet of paper. Ask a friend to hold up the paper thirty feet away. You will see not the dots but a straight line. In the same way, an able observer staring at faint detail on Mars might "see" lines where there were none.

At best, then, the *canali* are doubtful. More probably they do not exist.

The *canali* were one of the first things scientists looked for in the photographs taken by the United States space probe Mariner 4, which flew by Mars in 1965. The area that Mariner photographed was one in which several *canali* had been charted. Yet the photos showed no sign of them. (At the same time, it is true that Mariner photographed only about one percent of Mars' surface.)

Nor did the photos show any Earthlike features, such as mountain chains, valleys, or ocean basins. What they did show was a moonlike surface pitted with craters anything from 2 or 3 miles to 75 miles across. Scientists now think that Mars may have more than 10,000 large craters. These were probably formed over a very long period of time by the impact of meteorites. Like the moon's, these craters are both old and young.

The presence of so many craters means that there has been little, if any, weathering or upheaval on Mars. The craters have not crumbled under the upheaval of mountain-building or earthquakes. They

Spacecraft give us pictures of Mars unmatched by any telescope on Earth. These Mariner IV *photographs show*

the horizon of Mars from about 10,000 miles

and a closer view of the surface from about 8,000 miles.

75

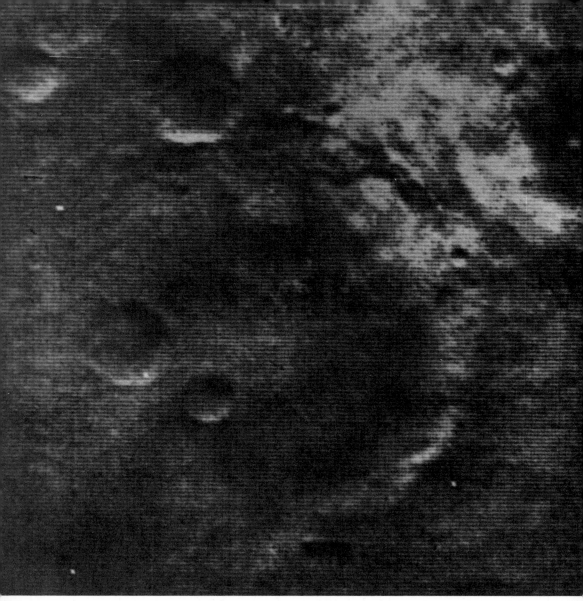

Photograph of Mars' surface taken by Mariner IV*, from about 8,000 miles above the surface*

have not been worn down by rivers, wind, or rain.

The lack of weathering fits with what scientists have found out about the atmosphere on Mars. It is much thinner and drier than the earth's. No rain falls on Mars, and its winds carry much less force than the earth's.

76

Scientists had long thought that the atmosphere must be very thin. But the Mariner fly-by showed that it was far thinner than anyone had thought. Atmospheric pressure is often measured in units called millibars. Surface pressure on the earth is 1,000 millibars. Scientists had thought the pressure on Mars was 85 millibars. Mariner's radio signals showed it to be 10 millibars.

Mars' atmosphere is made up chiefly of carbon dioxide and nitrogen. There seems to be methane. There is probably some argon in it. And there is a trace of water vapor. There may also be a trace of free oxygen, but none has so far been detected.

Because of the carbon dioxide, the atmosphere on Mars traps some heat from the sun. But because the atmosphere is so thin, much of the day's heat escapes by night. Temperatures on Mars may swing by as much as 180 degrees between day and night. Even in regions near the equator temperatures may drop far below freezing during the night.

The earth's atmosphere acts as a shield against certain dangerous radiations. The atmosphere on Mars does not, for it is very thin and it lacks ozone, which is a form of oxygen. There is an ozone layer in Earth's atmosphere that absorbs much of the ultraviolet radiation from the sun. This radiation would be fatal to most forms of life on Earth if it reached us in full force.

The earth's magnetic field traps still other dangerous radiation. This is made up of cosmic rays, which are high-energy particles coming from the sun and regions beyond. The particles that do get by the mag-

77

netic field strike the atmosphere and lose most of their energy before they reach the ground.

The Mariner fly-by reported that Mars does not seem to have a magnetic field—which probably means that the planet does not have a liquid core.

Mars, then, has little or no free oxygen. It has just a trace of water vapor in the air and a thin coating of ice on the ground. The atmospheric pressure is very low. Temperatures are below freezing much of the time. And the planet is showered with radiation that is dangerous to life as we know it.

Yet many scientists continue to think that life on Mars is possible. They say that life probably could not have developed on Mars in its present state. But they think that conditions on Mars were once much more favorable. They think that Mars may have had as much water as the earth. They are sure it must have had a much denser atmosphere. Because of the planet's weak gravity, much of the atmosphere escaped. As it evaporated, the water was also carried away. Higher forms of life, if there ever were any, must have died out. But it is possible that some primitive forms may have survived.

For, these scientists say, the evidence for simple, hardy plant life is very strong. They think that the dark regions on Mars can be nothing except living plants. How else, they ask, can we explain the changes in these regions? What else could change the shape of the regions? What else could account for the colors that change with the seasons?

A few scientists have replied that the dark regions could be lifeless and still show change. They might,

78

for example, consist of sand or minerals that change their color when wet.

That does not seem very likely, the other scientists argue. If the dark areas were lifeless, then the yellow sandstorms of Mars should long since have hidden them from view. As it is, the dark areas renew themselves each year. Surely they must be hardy, vigorous plants. Surviving cold, drought, and sandstorms, they come back each spring to make a quick and sweeping color change on the face of Mars.

What kind of plants might be growing on Mars? No one can say, for we know only the plants that grow on Earth. But what we know about these plants suggests that some forms of plant life might be able to survive under Martian conditions.

On our own planet there are plants that grow in extreme cold and in extreme drought. More that 60 species of lichens have been found growing on the stony peaks of a mountain range in Antarctica. An expedition to the Sahara studied soils whose moisture content was less than 0.5 per cent; in the soil samples, scientists found 98 species of bacteria, 28 species of fungi, and 84 species of algae.

On the rim of the Italian volcano Stromboli, scientists have collected tiny forms of life that not only live without oxygen but survive being frozen and then thawed out.

Then, too, very early forms of life on Earth were subjected to far more ultraviolet than we are today.

On our own planet certain kinds of life, such as bacteria, mosses, lichens, and algae, survive under extreme conditions. This may also be true of Mars.

79

But life on Mars could hardly be more than very simple and primitive. So far as we know, no kind of higher life could possibly exist on Mars today.

It will take manned or unmanned landings on Mars before we know for sure whether the red planet supports life. If it does, we may find that simple plants are the only kind of life that ever had a foothold on Mars. Or we may find that they are all that remain of many forms of life that once existed there.

7

The Asteroids: A Missing Planet?

A belt of space 340 million miles wide separates Mars from its outer neighbor, Jupiter. In that belt one of the strangest searches of modern astronomy took place nearly 200 years ago. It was a search for a missing planet. And it resulted in the discovery of hundreds of planets.

The story begins with a German astronomer named Johann Elert Bode. Like other astronomers, Bode knew that the distances separating the planets vary. Outward from the sun, these distances grow greater and greater. For example, there is a much bigger gap between the orbits of Jupiter and Saturn than between the orbits of Earth and Mars.

Studying these distances, Bode had observed a mathematical relationship among them. He developed a simple means of expressing it, which has come to be called Bode's Law.

The law is a quick and easy way of working out the relative distances of the planets from the sun. That is, it does not tell you how many miles a planet is from the sun. But it tells you that Mercury is less than half of Earth's distance from the sun, while Saturn is 10 times Earth's distance from the sun.

81

BODE'S LAW

(for estimating relative distances of planets from the sun)

			sums	Bode's distance	true distance
Mercury	0	4	4	0.4	0.39
Venus	3	4	7	0.7	0.72
Earth	6	4	10	1.0	1.00
Mars	12	4	16	1.6	1.52
X	24	4	28	2.8	2.70 (average)
Jupiter	48	4	52	5.2	5.20
Saturn	96	4	100	10.0	9.54
Uranus	192	4	196	19.6	19.19
Neptune	384	4	388	38.8	30.07
Pluto	768	4	772	77.2	39.46

Not known in Bode's time

How Bode's Law works: Beside the names of the planets, you write a series of numbers—0, 3, 6, 12, 24, and so on. You find the next number by doubling the one before (except in the case of zero).

Next, you add 4 to each number.

Then you divide each sum by 10; that is, you insert a decimal point before the last figure of each number. The result is the estimated relative distance of each planet from the sun as compared with Earth's distance (1.0). Venus, for example, is 0.7 of Earth's distance from the sun.

The final column of figures gives you the true relative distance. As you can see, the true distances are very close to Bode's, except for Neptune and Pluto. Some astronomers think that Pluto is not a true planet.

82

A meteorite found in Arizona

Bode found that his table worked very neatly except for one thing—the gap between Mars and Jupiter. There was no known planet between these two. To make the figures fit the facts, Bode would have had to omit number 2.8 from his series.

The law was not a theory. It did not attempt to explain anything. It simply summed up certain known facts. Still, it seemed curious that the law should work in every case but one. So Bode began to wonder about that gap between Mars and Jupiter. Mightn't it be possible that there was a planet there, one that hadn't been discovered?

Other astronomers agreed that the gap was strange. They began to search the sky, looking for an unknown planet. In fact, a group of German astronomers who called themselves Celestial Police set out to study every mile of space between Mars and Jupiter. But the first discovery was made by someone else. On the night of January 1, 1801, an Italian astronomer named Giuseppe Piazzi found a small celestial body in the belt of space between Mars and Jupiter. According to Bode's Law a planet in the belt should be 2.8 times the distance of Earth from the sun. Piazzi's find, which was later named Ceres, had a relative distance of 2.77.

Ceres, compared in size with the state of Texas

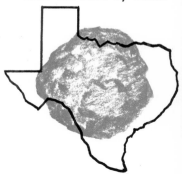

Ceres, however, had a diameter of only 480 miles. So astronomers began to wonder if this was really the planet predicted by Bode's Law. Thinking there might be something else in the gap, they again turned their telescopes on it. Sure enough—there was something else. A second little planet was discovered. This one, Pallas, was even smaller than Ceres. Soon after, two more were found: Juno and Vesta. Still others

83

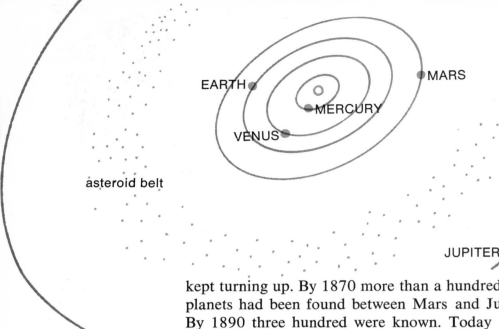

EARTH

MARS

MERCURY

VENUS

asteroid belt

JUPITER

The asteroid belt

kept turning up. By 1870 more than a hundred little planets had been found between Mars and Jupiter. By 1890 three hundred were known. Today about two thousand have been catalogued, and astronomers suspect that the total number may be fifty thousand. Ceres remains the largest, while the smallest ones observed are about the size of large rocks.

Because of their small size, they were not called planets but **asteroids**. Actually, this is not a very good name since it means "starlike bodies"—which is why you sometimes find them called **planetoids** ("planet-like bodies").

Most of the asteroids swing around the sun in orbits that lie between Mars and Jupiter. But some have orbits that carry them far out from that belt of space. A few swing out as far as Saturn's orbit. At least one passes closer to the sun than Mercury. Several tiny asteroids pass so close to the earth that they are known as "Earth-grazers." Apollo, for instance, passes within 7,000,000 miles of us; Adonis within 1,333,000 miles; and Hermes within 485,000 miles.

The asteroids are so small that a telescope shows them simply as points of light, and almost nothing is known about them. Even so, many people, perhaps including you, have probably touched pieces of one.

84

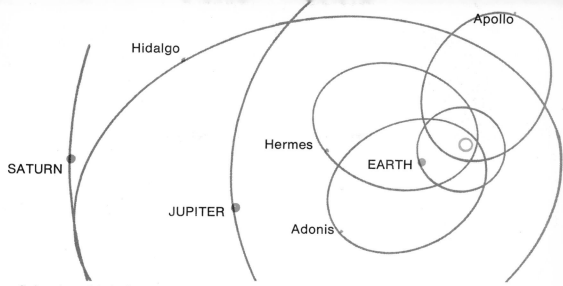

Scientists think that many of the meteorites that strike the earth are asteroids. Some of these meteorites are made of rock; some of an iron-nickel alloy; and some of both rock and the alloy. To the best of our knowledge the earth is made of these same materials. And if all the planets were born at the same time in the same cloud of dust and gas, then all are probably made of the same materials.

Are the asteroids, then, fragments of a lost planet? Or are they a planet that never formed?

The newest evidence strongly suggests that they are a planet that never formed. This evidence is based on a chemical study of certain elements in meteorites. The study shows that during most of their existence the meteorites remained at a temperature of minus 121 degrees Fahrenheit. This indicates two things:

They have never been closer to the sun than 140 million miles, about the distance of the asteroid belt. Otherwise the sun's rays would have heated them up.

They have never been part of an object with a diameter greater than 100 miles. If they had been part of a large planet, that planet's radioactivity would have heated them up.

If this is so, how can the asteroids be explained?

Some scientists suggest that Jupiter's strong gravitational field prevented a planet from forming in

A few asteroids do not stay within the asteroid belt. One of these is Hermes. Hermes sometimes passes very close to the earth's orbit. It once came within 485,000 miles of the earth. It is one of the asteroids known as Earth-grazers. Apollo and Adonis are two other Earth-grazers. Hidalgo also leaves the belt. It swings out as far as the orbit of Saturn. Several asteroids travel in Jupiter's orbit.

A few asteroids leave space. They become meteorites. If you have ever touched a meteorite, like the one on Page 83, you may have touched an asteroid.

85

what is now the asteroid belt. Perhaps the material that might have become a planet simply turned into the asteroids. Perhaps it formed a number of small planets that collided with one another and shattered.

However, an earlier theory holds that the asteroids are fragments of a lost planet. Long ago, this theory states, a violent accident shattered the planet with a force that must have lighted up the whole solar system. After the accident, a fearsome Age of Meteorites began, when gigantic fireballs blasted vast holes in the crust of the earth and other planets.

What could shatter a whole planet into fragments? There are three main theories about this:

(1) The missing planet was destroyed by Jupiter. Scientists know that a large planet can destroy a body that is less massive and less dense than itself. This happens when the smaller body passes into a certain part of the larger planet's gravitational field. There it is torn apart by the force of that field. Perhaps the missing planet was drawn closer and closer to Jupiter until at last it was shattered.

(2) The missing planet exploded by itself. There is a possibility that radioactivity within the planet created enough pressure to make it explode like a bomb.

(3) It was the victim of a collision. Perhaps it collided with one of Jupiter's moons. Perhaps it collided with something else. One theory supposes that there were two small planets in orbit between Mars and Jupiter and that these two came together in collision.

Precisely what happened remains one of the great mysteries of astronomy. And if mighty Jupiter was the "villain," that planet guards its secret well.

86

8

Jupiter and Saturn

Beyond the asteroids lie four giant planets: Jupiter, Saturn, Uranus, and Neptune. They are very different from the inner planets, which are basically balls of rock surrounded by a little gas. The giant outer planets appear to be mostly atmosphere. Each is wrapped in dense clouds and layers of gases that are thousands of miles deep. Very little is known about any of them.

In the beginning probably all the planets looked like today's giants. But the sun's heat warmed the atmospheres of the inner planets, and most of the gases escaped into space. On the outer planets this did not happen. Lying far from the sun, they still hold the gases of their original atmospheres. These gases are chiefly hydrogen, ammonia, methane and probably helium.

The outer planet we know best is Jupiter. Named

JUPITER

average diameter	86,800 miles
average distance from sun	483,300,000 miles
average speed of revolution	29,400 miles per hour
length of year	almost 12 earth years
length of day	almost 10 earth hours
gravity	2.64 of Earth's
temperature at top of atmosphere	$-200°$ F.
moons	12

after the greatest of the Roman gods, Jupiter is a giant among giants, with a diameter almost eleven times that of the earth. Besides being the biggest planet in our solar system, Jupiter is the giant closest to the earth. Its distance from us varies between 365 million and 600 million miles. This may not seem exactly "close," but Jupiter is so big and bright that it can easily be seen without a telescope. Through only a small telescope, it appears as big as the moon does to the unaided eye.

Swinging around a nearly circular orbit, Jupiter

88

takes almost 12 earth years to complete one trip about the sun. But if Jupiter's year is long, its day is short. The big planet rotates once in just under 10 hours. That rapid rate of spinning has given Jupiter the shape of a slightly flattened ball.

Like the other giants, Jupiter is far less dense than the small inner planets. The explanation is that the huge disk we see is atmosphere, while the core of the planet is much smaller. Astronomers think that the core may have a diameter of 37,400 miles, which would make it about five times as large as the earth.

No one, however, knows what the core is like. For a long time many scientists thought that it must be cold. They thought that the core might be rock covered with vast oceans of ice or that it might be gas under such great pressure that it was as dense as metal. Today many scientists think that the core may be generating a great deal of heat. Most of the heat that the earth generates is caused by radioactivity in the earth's interior, although some may also be generated by gravitational contraction. Since Jupiter is much more massive than the earth, its interior may produce much more heat. It may generate so much heat that the surface of the planet is molten.

Other scientists suggest a different source of heat. It is true, they say, that Jupiter is so far from the sun that it does not receive much heat. But its atmosphere is so dense that the heat it does receive may be trapped at the planet's surface and accumulate. The lower layers of the atmosphere may be about 70 degrees and the surface of the planet may be covered with warm seas of ammonia or even water.

A few scientists have gone even further. They say

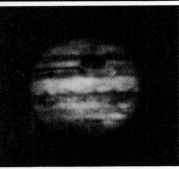

Three views of Jupiter showing the movement of the Red Spot

that Jupiter's atmosphere may be very much like that of the earth at the time life first developed. Possibly life has also developed on Jupiter. These scientists have found on Earth some bacteria and fungi that seem to thrive in an artifically created atmosphere of methane, ammonia, and hydrogen. Perhaps, the scientists say, life is developing in parts of Jupiter's atmosphere where the density and temperature are right.

Someday a space probe may tell us what Jupiter is like, but for now scientists can see and study only the top of the atmosphere. It is mysterious marked with broad, colored bands and a huge colored spot. These markings have puzzled astronomers ever since they were first seen through a telescope.

The planet's atmosphere is divided into a number of bands, each several thousand miles wide. They appear as wide belts of color—pink, tan, yellow, green-blue or gray. Generally speaking, the bands have been growing duller in color during the past thirty years. But why they should change color at all, no one knows. The bands change in other ways, too. Sometimes they widen or narrow or even disappear for a time.

Their rates of rotation vary. Around Jupiter's equator is a belt 10,000 to 15,000 miles wide; it rotates once every 9 hours and 50 minutes. Other bands take 5 or 6 minutes longer.

In addition to the bands, astronomers have observed light spots and dark spots and other markings in the atmosphere of Jupiter. All of these also change, and many of them appear only to disappear after a brief time.

90

THE FOUR BIG MOONS OF JUPITER

NAME	DIAMETER IN MILES	MILES FROM JUPITER
Io	2,000	262,000
Europa	1,800	417,000
Ganymede	3,100	666,000
Callisto	2,800	1,170,000

The best known of the markings is the great Red Spot, which astronomers have been studying since 1831. The Red Spot is some 30,000 miles long and 7,000 miles wide. Over the years its color has changed from brick red to pink to pale gray. Sometimes the Red Spot is easy to see, while at other times it is almost invisible. No one knows what it is.

The Red Spot moves around Jupiter at different speeds, sometimes slowing down and sometimes speeding up. This seems to prove that it cannot be attached to Jupiter's surface; if it were, it would move at a constant speed. The Red Spot may be a solid body of some sort, perhaps a gigantic lump of frozen ammonia, floating in a sea of gas. Or it may be a peculiar cloud formation caused by a mountain on the planet's surface that disturbs the flow of air above it.

Another very strange thing about Jupiter is that it sends out great bursts of radio waves. For some years astronomers thought that the radio waves were caused by lightning during huge thunderstorms. Today they are not so sure. Certain bursts of radio waves always come from the same parts of Jupiter. This suggests that the cause is on the planet's surface.

When it comes to Jupiter's satellites, astronomers find themselves on more familiar ground. As far as we know, Jupiter has twelve moons, most of which are solid bodies.

The four biggest moons—Io, Europa, Ganymede, and Callisto—were discovered by Galileo. Io, which is about the size of our moon, appears to be a globe of rock mixed with metal. Some people see it as orange in color; others see it as light yellow or white. Europa

91

appears generally white. At times it seems to have light polar regions and a dark belt circling the equator. Ganymede, which is a little bigger than Mercury, looks rather like Mars. It has polar caps, a yellow-orange surface marked with dark patches, and some canal-like lines. Though almost as big as Ganymede, Callisto is hard to see since it is both a great distance from us and a poor reflector of light. In the telescope Callisto appears blue-gray. If this is its true color, then the big moon must be different from the other three. Astronomers suspect that it may be either a solid ball of ice or a ball of rock covered with ice.

For 280 years after Galileo's discovery, astronomers thought of Jupiter as having only four moons. Then, starting in 1892, various astronomers began discovering still more moons circling the giant planet. The eighth additional moon was discovered in 1951.

All eight are small: their diameters range from 20 to 150 miles. One is only 113,000 miles from Jupiter, so close that it may some day be destroyed by the planet's gravitational field. The four farthest out are between 13 million and 14 million miles from Jupiter. They are peculiar because they revolve around Jupiter from east to west. The other eight moons revolve from west to east. Perhaps the four distant moons were asteroids that were captured by Jupiter.

Human explorers will probably never wish to go closer to Jupiter than its outermost moons. Scientists report that the giant planet is surrounded by a vast sea of deadly radiation. Trapped by Jupiter's magnetic field, this sea is thought to be a million times bigger than the one surrounding Earth and 100 to 1,000 times as deadly.

92

Possibly a way will be found to shield explorers from such radiation. Even so, it is doubtful if they would attempt a landing on Jupiter. At the top of the atmosphere they would find temperatures of minus 200 degrees and gases that would ice up their spaceship. On the way down they would probably pass through violent thunderstorms. The surface may prove to be molten. If they could land on it, they would be subjected to air pressure perhaps 200,000 times as great as the earth's. The pull of Jupiter's gravity would make movement extremely difficult. And tremendous rocket power would be required for an escape from Jupiter. For men, this giant planet is a forbidding and alien world.

Saturn, the next planet out from the sun, is in many ways very much like Jupiter. Saturn, too, is an immense planet, probably circled by a sea of deadly radiation. Its surface is hidden from us by a deep, dense atmosphere. The atmosphere is probably made up of the same gases as Jupiter's, and the core of the planet is also likely to be the same as Jupiter's. Saturn even shows colored bands and other markings similar to Jupiter's at the top of its atmosphere. Though they are less bright in their coloring, they are probably caused in the same ways as Jupiter's.

Like Jupiter, Saturn has a number of moons. Ten are known, and more may be found. The tenth, which is named Janus, was discovered in 1967. It is a small moon, 100 to 200 miles in diameter.

Another of the moons, Titan, is huge. It is about the same size as Mercury. Planet-sized, it has an atmosphere of its own, probably of methane. Titan's

Saturn and its innermost moons

surface may be a mass of methane glaciers. But that is just a guess. The big moon is so far away that it appears in the telescope only as a yellow-orange disk marked with two dark patches.

Almost nothing is known about the other moons of Saturn. The inner ones may be worlds of ice—of frozen water and ammonia. Apart from this, we can only guess that the moon called Phoebe may be an asteroid captured by Saturn. Like the outer moons of Jupiter, Phoebe circles its planet from east to west; Saturn's other moons move from west to east.

But Saturn is not Jupiter's identical twin. Smaller than Jupiter, it is almost twice as far from the sun. For that reason, it travels a longer orbit at a slower speed, taking 29½ earth years to circle the sun. But, like Jupiter, Saturn spins very rapidly on its axis. It rotates once in about 10 hours, and therefore is slightly flattened in shape.

Still, these are minor differences. There is one other thing that not only sets Saturn off from Jupiter but also makes it unique in the solar system. Saturn is circled by rings that spread out some 41,000 miles from the planet.

Seen with the unaided eye, Saturn appears as a not very bright planet. The rings that make it both beautiful and spectacular cannot be seen. It takes a telescope to bring the rings into view. And so it happened that Galileo was the first man to see them, though he could not make out what they were. As seen through his telescope, Saturn seemed to have a bulging shape. Galileo at first thought the bulges were caused by two motionless moons. But when the "moons" vanished from sight one night, as the rings

94

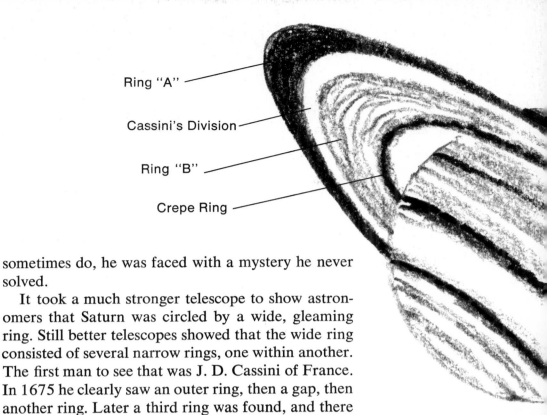

Ring "A"

Cassini's Division

Ring "B"

Crepe Ring

sometimes do, he was faced with a mystery he never solved.

It took a much stronger telescope to show astronomers that Saturn was circled by a wide, gleaming ring. Still better telescopes showed that the wide ring consisted of several narrow rings, one within another. The first man to see that was J. D. Cassini of France. In 1675 he clearly saw an outer ring, then a gap, then another ring. Later a third ring was found, and there may be still others.

The rings are difficult to see in detail chiefly because they are so far away. Also, since Saturn's axis is tilted at about 27 degrees, we do not always have the same view of them. Sometimes we see the rings from above, sometimes from below. At certain times they face us edge on, and they are then so thin that we cannot see them.

Once Saturn's rings had been seen, astronomers began to wonder what they were made of. Were they a gas, a solid, or a liquid? The British scientist Clerk Maxwell answered this question in 1857. He showed that the rings could not be either a gas or a liquid, for then they would break apart. Instead, he said, the rings must be composed of a vast number of tiny particles that orbit Saturn.

Today's astronomers agree. They say the particles in the rings are tiny "moons," ranging in size from

95

SATURN

average diameter	71,500 miles
average distance from sun	886,200,000 miles
average speed of revolution	21,700 miles per hour
length of year	$29\frac{1}{2}$ earth years
length of day	about 10 earth hours
gravity	1.17 of Earth's
temperature in atmosphere	$-220°$ F.
moons	10 known

specks of dust to baseballs. Each particle revolves around Saturn in its own orbit. Since the particles reflect a good deal of light, it's probable that each one is encased in ice or frost. They may even be snowballs formed of ice crystals in some way we do not understand. However, it is more likely that the particles are tiny pieces of rock covered with ice. Perhaps the rock was left over at the time Saturn formed. Perhaps Saturn once had another satellite that circled closer and closer, into the danger zone of the planet's gravitational field. When the satellite was shattered, the rings formed out of its remains.

If that is so, then the remains spell danger for future space travelers. Not all the particles would be in the rings. Many would be wandering about the planet in odd orbits, forming a swarm of small satellites. Moving at meteroic speed, they would wreck any spaceship that blundered into their field.

Saturn, one of the most dangerous planets for space travelers, was the outermost planet known to the ancients. Through most of history, men thought that beyond Saturn there was only empty space reaching out to the stars.

But, as we now know, there were more planets sweeping around in lonely paths billions of miles from the sun. Of them, only one can be seen without a telescope. This is Uranus, first of the outermost planets to be discovered.

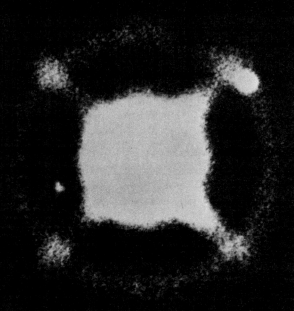

URANUS

average diameter	29,400 miles
average distance from sun	1,783,000,000 miles
average speed of revolution	15,310 miles per hour
length of year	about 84 earth years
length of day	10¾ earth hours
gravity	1.09 of Earth's
temperature near surface	$-200°$ F.
moons	5

9

Uranus, Neptune, and Pluto

The man who discovered Uranus was William Herschel, an English organist who was also an amateur astronomer.

In the winter of 1780-81, Herschel finished building a new seven-inch reflecting telescope and began to study the stars through it. On the night of March 13, he had his telescope turned on the constellation of Gemini. There to his great surprise he found an extra "star." An excellent astronomer, Herschel was quick to realize that what he had found could not be a star, for it appeared in his telescope as a glowing disk rather than a twinkling point of light. Continuing to observe his find night after night, Herschel discovered that it was moving among the stars of Gemini. Finally he decided that he had discovered a new **comet** and wrote up a detailed report of his observations.

Uranus and its five moons. The ring and rays were made by the telescope lens.

99

The report of a new comet excited astronomers all over Europe, and they eagerly trained their telescopes on Herschel's discovery. But the more they studied it, the more they began to wonder if it really was a comet. For one thing, it seemed to be following a nearly circular orbit out beyond Saturn. Finally it became clear that Herschel had discovered not a comet but a planet. Checking their records, astronomers found that the planet had been sighted twenty times in the preceding hundred years but that each time it had been dismissed as a faint star. These earlier sightings, however, proved a great help later in plotting the orbit of the newly discovered planet.

In keeping with the names of the other planets, Uranus was called after the god of the sky, perhaps because it was then the most distant planet known. Uranus lies nearly 2 billion miles from the sun—19 times farther away than the earth. At that great distance, it is difficult to observe. The telescope shows Uranus only as a pale green disk with some fuzzy markings rather like Saturn's. Its brightness seems to vary as it moves in its distant orbit.

Traveling with Uranus are five moons, two of which were discovered by Herschel. They, of course, are even harder to see than their planet. Astronomers think their diameters measure from about 200 miles to 1,000 miles. The distances separating them from Uranus range from perhaps 75,000 to 365,000 miles.

The diameter of Uranus itself is about 29,400 miles, which makes it the third largest planet in the solar system. It takes 84 earth years to travel round its orbit. But its day, like those of the other giants, is short: 10 hours and 45 minutes.

100

Uranus and three of its moons

The odd thing about Uranus is the tilt of its axis, with respect to the plane of its orbit. The other planets are tilted somewhere between 3 degrees and 29 degrees. Uranus is tilted 98 degrees.

From our point of view, this means that sometimes we see Uranus with its north pole pointing at us. At other times we see it with its equatorial belt running up and down instead of across. The tilt also means that viewed from beyond its north pole Uranus would appear to be rotating clockwise as it moves around its orbit.

Uranus is so far from us that almost nothing is known about it. There is a large amount of methane in its atmosphere. Hydrogen is also present and so, probably, is helium. If the atmosphere ever had ammonia gas, carbon dioxide, or water vapor, these have been frozen out of the atmosphere by its low temperature. Distant Uranus receives almost no light and heat from the sun yet new research shows that the temperatures near its surface are about minus 200 degrees. The planet may have a source of internal heat.

It was Uranus that led astronomers, sixty-five years later, to Neptune, fourth and last of the giant planets. The discovery came about this way:

By plotting the path of a planet, astronomers can draw up tables that show them exactly where the planet will be at any given time. So, after the discovery of Uranus, they set about plotting its orbit. But for once the method didn't seem to work. Sometimes Uranus turned up ahead of its predicted position; sometimes it was behind.

101

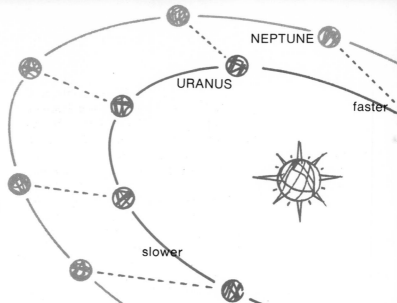

NEPTUNE

URANUS

faster

slower

So astronomers began to think that perhaps another planet lay beyond Uranus. Perhaps its gravitational field was affecting the motion of Uranus. Perhaps that was the explanation of Uranus' odd behavior. For, as astronomers knew, planets do influence one another's motions.

Not until the 1840's did anyone attempt to put that idea to the test. Then, as so often happens in science, two men attacked the problem at the same time without knowing of each other's work. Both solved it. In England, young John C. Adams, only just out of college, proved by mathematics that there must be a planet beyond Uranus and indicated where it might be found. In France, the astronomer Urbain Leverrier also solved the problem.

Both Adams and Leverrier appealed to their fellow astronomers for help in locating the planet.

In England, James Challis searched for the planet during the summer of 1846. Following Adams' directions, he saw the new planet through his telescope—and failed to recognize it.

In the fall of that year, a German astronomer named Johann G. Galle received a letter from Leverrier concerning the unseen planet. The letter arrived on September 23, 1846. Following its directions,

102

As Uranus overtakes Neptune, it is affected by Neptune's gravitational pull and moves faster in its orbit. As it moves ahead, Uranus slows down because Neptune acts as a brake. This unexpected speeding up and slowing down puzzled astronomers until they realized that there was another planet, orbiting beyond Uranus. This led to the search for Neptune which was finally located in 1846.

Galle found the planet that very night. Since it appeared pale green in color, the new planet was named Neptune, after the god of the sea.

Unlike Uranus, Neptune can be seen only through a telescope. Astronomers report that it has a light band around the equator and that its polar regions are dimmer than the rest of it. That is all the detail that even the most powerful telescopes reveal.

Neptune is the smallest of the giant planets. Its diameter is more than a third of Jupiter's (but nearly four times that of the earth). As the most distant of the giants, Neptune is the slowest moving. It takes 164¾ earth years to make one trip around the sun. It also spins more slowly than the other big planets. It seems to rotate about once every 15¾ hours.

Neptune is nearly three billion miles from the sun. At that distance there is hardly any difference between daylight and darkness. Neptune is a dark world in a cold part of the solar system. At the top of its atmosphere temperatures are about 330 degrees below zero. Yet astronomers say that Neptune has a warm region thousands of miles down in its atmosphere. The gases in its atmosphere are probably the same as those in the atmosphere of Uranus.

So far, astronomers have found only two moons

103

NEPTUNE

average diameter	31,250 miles
average distance from sun	2,794,000,000 miles
average speed of revolution	12,240 miles per hour
length of year	164¾ earth years
length of day	15¾ earth hours?
gravity	1.12 of Earth's
average temperature at top of atmosphere	$-330°$ F.
moons	2

Neptune and its two moons

circling Neptune. Nereid is tiny, perhaps 200 miles in diameter, and its distance from Neptune is about 3,500,000 miles. Triton, the other, is huge, a giant among moons. Astronomers have not managed to measure it accurately, but they think its diameter is probably about 2,350 miles. This big moon is only 220,000 miles from Neptune, about the distance of our own moon from Earth. But in the dim light

104

Triton, as seen from its planet, would appear only as a dull gray globe hanging in nearby space.

At first the discovery of Neptune seemed to account nicely for the changes in Uranus' speed. Since Uranus traveled inside Neptune's orbit, there came a time when it overtook its outer neighbor. Approaching, Uranus was pulled along faster by Neptune's gravity. Passing, Uranus was braked and slowed down by Neptune's gravity.

But as time went by, astronomers plotted positions and checked their figures. And Uranus still didn't always turn up exactly where it should have been. Was there yet another planet? Was it disturbing Uranus' motion?

Percival Lowell decided that there had to be another planet—an unseen ninth. Like Adams and Leverrier, he sought the planet by using mathematics and based his calculations on what was known about Uranus' orbit. By 1905 he had worked out where Planet X might be found. But he did not publish his prediction until 1915, a year before his death. At Harvard College Observatory another astronomer, W. H. Pickering, also plotted the position of Planet X. He based his figures on how the unseen planet affected Uranus and Neptune. Both Lowell and Pickering believed that Planet X would be found in a certain area of the sky.

Knowing that the planet would be faint and hard to see among the many stars, Lowell searched for it with a telescopic camera. He was looking for a point of light that appeared to move among the fixed stars. But the cameras available were not up to the job. The search had to be abandoned.

Some years later it was taken up again by a young, self-taught astronomer named Clyde Tombaugh. In 1928, using the telescope he had built on his father's farm, Tombaugh spent many nights studying Mars and recording his observations. To see how his drawings compared with those of experts, he sent them to the Lowell Observatory. The director was so impressed with the young man's work that he offered him a job. The job was that of photographic assistant in the search for Planet X.

By the time Tombaugh set to work, the observatory had some new and important equipment. There was a 13-inch telescope with a wide field—one that could cover a large area of sky. There was also a blink microscope. It was used to compare photos taken on successive nights.

Tombaugh's job required him to work with both instruments. With the telescopic camera he photographed the same region of sky several nights apart. With the blink microscope he compared pairs of matched plates. Painstakingly he checked star against star, seeking among many distant points of light the tiny shifting one that might be Planet X. For a year he worked without success.

Then on February 18, 1930, Tombaugh was comparing the plates of January 23 and 29. In them he noted a dot that had shifted its position. Was this Planet X?

It was. The observatory's big telescope showed it as a dim light moving through the distant sky on a steady course. Planet X had been found.

It was called Pluto, after the god of darkness. The name was a fitting choice. The new planet was a dark

106

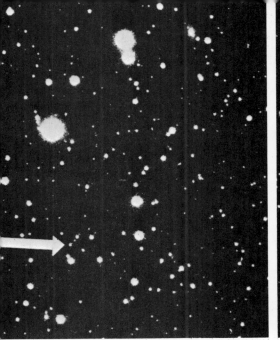

PLUTO

average diameter	3,600 miles?
average distance from sun	3,670,000,000 miles
average speed of revolution	10,800 miles per hour
length of year	about 248 earth years
length of day	6½ earth days?
gravity	?
temperature	−350° F. ?
moons	?

world. And the first two letters of Pluto were the initials of Percival Lowell, the man who first predicted the planet's existence.

Lowell, a brilliant mathematician, had come very close to describing Pluto exactly:

(1) He had predicted a small planet. Pluto is small: its diameter is less than half that of the earth.

(2) He had predicted that Planet X would require 282 years to journey once around its orbit. Pluto makes one revolution in about 248 years.

(3) He had predicted that Planet X would be found 4 billion miles from the sun. Pluto's average distance is just a little less than that.

Clyde Tombaugh's examination of these two photographs, taken on January 23 and 29, 1930, led to the discovery of Pluto (shown by the arrows).

107

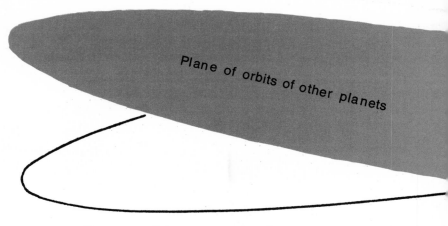

Plane of orbits of other planets

Because of its enormous distance from the sun, Pluto travels through endless night, receiving almost no heat or light from the sun. And the sun, as seen from Pluto, would be simply another bright star.

Pluto is so far from the earth that it is extremely difficult to observe. In the most powerful telescope it appears only as a dim yellowish dot. No markings can be seen. If Pluto has moons, astronomers do not see them. Nor can they see Pluto spinning, though they guess it may have a rotation period of 6½ days.

Since Pluto is a poor reflector of light, its surface is probably made up of dark-colored materials. And it must be extremely cold, perhaps minus 350 degrees Fahrenheit.

Beyond these few facts almost nothing is known about Pluto, and some of the "facts" are really guesses. Astronomers are certain only of Pluto's orbit and its smallness. But that is enough to prove that Pluto is a very odd sort of planet.

For one thing, it is too small to be one of the family of outer planets. In size Pluto resembles the inner planets, which do not have atmospheres thousands of miles deep. It does not seem to belong with the giants.

Yet, small as it is, Pluto appears to influence the motions of both Uranus and Neptune. If it is really doing this, it must be extremely dense with a very strong gravitational field. Its density would have to be 10 times that of the earth—or 5 times that of lead.

108

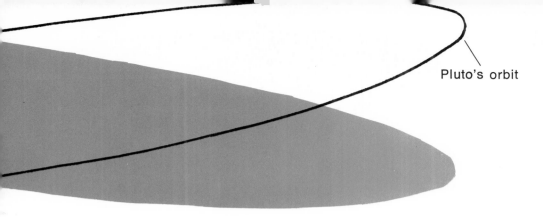

Pluto's orbit

This is out of keeping with everything known about our solar system.

Then there is Pluto's orbit, which has two odd things about it.

First, it is not in the same plane as the orbits of the other planets. If you could stand on the sun and sight along the orbits of the planets, you would see that they all lined up with one another pretty well —except for Pluto's.

Second, at times Pluto swings inside Neptune's orbit. It moves toward a point where it is 35 million miles nearer to the sun than Neptune is. This is shown in the drawing of the solar system at the beginning of this book.

These facts make some astronomers doubt that Pluto is a true planet. That is, they do not believe that Pluto was born a planet. They think that Pluto was originally one of Neptune's satellites. Escaping from its planet, Pluto began to orbit the sun.

Perhaps there is another giant planet circling in the dark, billions of miles from the sun and as yet undiscovered. But it is much more likely that Neptune is the last of the true planets and that beyond it, at the far reaches of the solar system, there are only comets, Pluto, and possibly some other escaped satellites.

Certainly, when seen against the order of the solar system, Pluto does not behave like a true planet. Nor does it fit well into the theory that most astronomers think explains the birth of the planets.

109

10

The Birth of the Planets

Measured against the long history of astronomy, man's understanding of the solar system is fairly recent. The fact that there is such a thing as the solar system was first understood only in the 1600's and 1700's, through the work of Copernicus, Galileo, Newton, and other great scientists. Then astronomers began to see that the sun and planets form one big family. The family is a unit in space and its members obey certain laws. That is, there is a pattern to the solar system. As you remember:

Generally speaking, the members of the solar system move counter-clockwise. Seen from the north, the sun rotates counter-clockwise. This is also the direction in which the planets move around the sun in elliptical orbits.

110

Except for Pluto's, the orbits of the planets lie on nearly the same plane.

In general, the planets are separated in an orderly way (Bode's Law).

The planets can be divided into two distinct classes: small solid bodies and giants wrapped in thick atmospheres.

This broad pattern indicates that all the planets must have been formed at about the same time and in the same way. It indicates, too, that their birth was somehow related to the sun.

For some two hundred years scientists have been working out theories to explain the birth of the planets. Each major theory has sought to account for the pattern of the solar system. And each has stemmed from one of two basic ideas:

(1) The planets were born in a great cloud of dust and gas, as was the sun.

(2) The planets came directly from the sun.

The first important theory about the birth of the planets was published in 1755 by Immanuel Kant, a German philosopher.

According to Kant, the sun and planets had formed out of a huge, thin cloud of dust and gas. Two forces were at work in the cloud. One was the tendency of heavier matter to move toward the cloud's center. The second was the tendency of the cloud to expand. The cloud began to rotate. Gradually, it flattened into a big disk. (The central part of the disk became the sun.)

Within the spinning disk, particles of gas and dust attracted one another. Drawn together, they formed

111

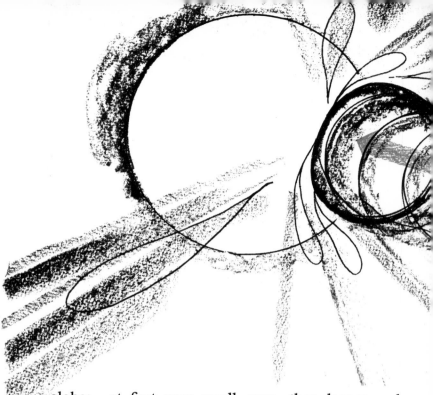

globes—at first very small ones, then larger and larger globes. Finally, matter was packed so tightly around the cores of the globes that they began to give off heat. The globes became huge, hot, molten spheres. Cooling over millions of years, they eventually became the planets and their satellites.

In his own day, Kant's theory did not cause much of a stir among scientists. But today's scientists find much merit in it, except for his explanation of the forces that set the cloud spinning.

Some twenty years later, a very different idea was suggested by a great French scientist, the Comte de Buffon. In 1778 he published his collision theory.

According to this theory, the sun had formed alone. The planets were born much later, when the sun was hit by a comet. (By "comet" modern scientists think that Buffon probably meant "another star.") Because of the collision, billions of tons of matter from the sun were splashed into space. As time went on, this matter collected into globes. The

112

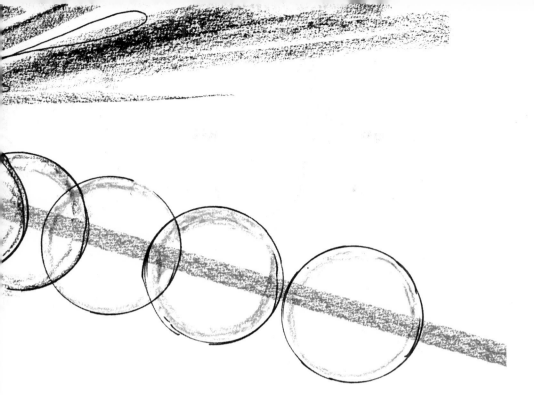

globes contracted and generated heat. Much later they cooled into the planets we know.

Buffon's theory of the birth of the planets

Buffon's theory didn't excite much interest either. But the next explanation of the birth of the planets did. It was published in 1796 by a French astronomer named Pierre Simon de Laplace. An expanded and revised version of Kant's idea, it was generally accepted as true for a hundred years.

Laplace imagined that the birth of our solar system began with the tremendous explosion of a star. Exploding, the star expanded, creating a vast fiery mist of gas and dust that reached far out beyond what we know as the limits of the solar system. The fiery mist of gases whirled round its center. After a while the mist began to cool and contract. Because it was contracting, it spun faster and faster.

The spinning mist threw off great rings of gas. The first ring lay far out, about where the orbit of the farthest-known planet is. The second ring lay within that, the third within the second, and so on.

113

Laplace's theory In time the rings cooled and began to contract, forming more or less solid planets. As they did so, they, too, threw off rings, which became their moons. Meanwhile, the center of the mist had contracted into the glowing globe that became our sun.

Scientists of Laplace's day liked his theory because it seemed to account for the pattern of the solar system. It even explained why the outer planets were bigger than the inner planets and had more moons: the first few rings thrown off would have been the most massive ones.

Later scientists found two weaknesses in the theory. A major criticism came from Clerk Maxwell, the British scientist who had solved the mystery of Saturn's rings. He said that rings thrown off by the whirling cloud could not have become planets. They would have stayed rings, just as Saturn's rings have stayed rings. A second criticism has to do with the speeds of rotation in the solar system. Most of the planets rotate faster than the sun. But this would be

114

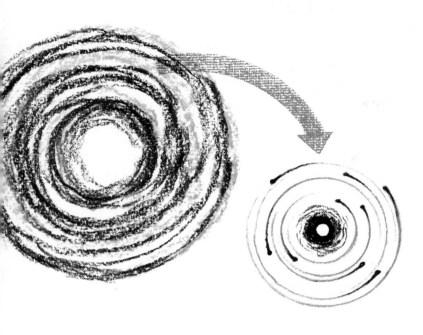

impossible if the cloud-sun had thrown off ring-planets. There is no way in which the sun could give the planets a faster speed of rotation than it has itself.

So in the late 1800's a number of scientists dropped the Kant-Laplace idea. They turned back to Buffon's theory and began to revise it.

The first important revision was put forward around 1900 by two American scientists, F. R. Moulton, an astronomer, and T. C. Chamberlin, a geologist. Their idea is often called the **planetesimal** theory; a planetesimal is a tiny planet or a very small heavenly body that moves in a regular orbit.

As you may know, all stars travel very rapidly through space. Moulton and Chamberlin suggested that, several billion years ago, another star sped very close to our sun. Its gravitational force raised two great tides, one on either side of the sun. As Star X passed our sun, the top part of a tidal bulge was torn off and hurled into space.

115

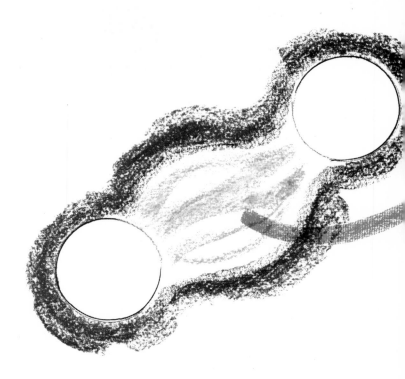

When Star X had passed, some of the material that had been torn loose was drawn back into the sun. But most of it became a great flat ring that circled the sun. Over a period of many years, the gas in the ring cooled and became liquid. Then the liquid changed to small solid masses—the planetesimals. Larger planetesimals kept sweeping up smaller ones, growing and growing. And in this way the planets were formed.

(Naturally, what happened to the sun also happened to Star X. If the theory proved true, Star X would also have a family of planets.)

About eighteen years later, a different version of this theory was worked out by two British scientists, Sir James Jeans and Harold Jeffreys. In general, they agreed with the two American scientists. But they did not believe that the planets could have formed from planetesimals.

Jeans and Jeffreys said that Star X either had

116

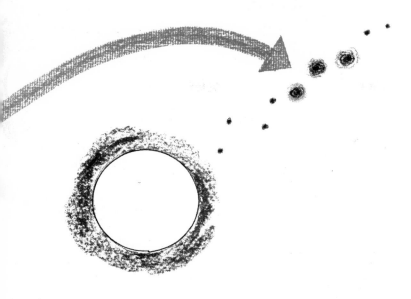

passed very close to the sun or had actually grazed *Jeans' theory* the sun. As a result, matter was pulled out of both stars. It was not a disk but cigar-shaped. That is, it was thickest in the middle and tapered toward the ends. Gradually, the matter in the "cigar" began to solidify into globes. The giant planets formed in the thick section. The small planets formed at the ends.

The Jeans-Jeffreys theory solved certain problems that the Moulton-Chamberlin theory did not. But both shared certain weaknesses. For one thing, they did not really account for the pattern of the solar system. For another, both were based on the very slim chance of a collision between stars. Space is so vast that even a near collision would be a rare event. Jeans himself calculated that one could take place only once in billions of years.

So other scientists continued to work on other theories. One theory suggests that the planets formed out of matter from an exploding star. Perhaps that

117

star had once been our sun's partner in a double-star system. Perhaps our sun and the exploding star were born together in a whole shower of stars.

In a way, that idea is much more probable, for exploding stars are fairly common. But some astronomers rule out these theories. They say the planets could not have formed from matter contained in a star. Such matter would be thousands of degrees hot near the surface. Its swiftly moving molecules would spread out into space and be lost before there was time for planets to form.

Most modern astronomers have now turned back to the very first scientific theory, Kant's. Looked at in the light of modern knowledge, it seems very promising.

For many years, there was one major argument against Kant's theory: it wouldn't work. What Maxwell had said about Laplace's theory also applied to Kant's: the great flat disk of gas and dust could not turn into planets. It would simply remain a disk.

Today we know this argument does not hold true. The reason has to do with the chemical composition of the universe.

In Maxwell's time, scientists thought the whole universe was made of the same matter we know on earth. That meant the most abundant elements would be oxygen, silicon, iron, and other elements found on the earth. Now scientists know that is not so. The sun and other stars are 99 percent hydrogen and helium with only 1 percent of the other elements.

So the great flat disk that formed around the sun must also have been mostly hydrogen and helium. If that is so, the mass of the disk was much greater than

118

Maxwell thought. In a more massive disk, the forces of gravity would have been much stronger. They would have been strong enough to cause the break-up of the disk. Once that happened, planets could have formed.

It was Carl von Weizsäcker, a German scientist, who first showed that Maxwell's argument did not hold up. With that argument destroyed, there was much to be said for Kant's theory. Von Weizsäcker revised it. And his theory has since been revised by Gerard P. Kuiper, George Gamow, and other scientists. Kant's theory, brought up to date, is the one favored by most scientists today. You read a description of it at the beginning of this book.

It supposes that about five billion years ago the sun and planets began to form out of a vast, thin-spread cloud of gas and dust.

The cloud particles were moving, and they also tended to attract one another. They moved closer together, and so the cloud began to condense. As it condensed, the force of gravity at its center grew stronger and stronger. Material streamed inward, slowly at first, then faster and faster. Eventually the cloud collapsed in on itself. It formed a huge ball of gas and dust that began to spin.

Spinning, the ball flattened into a great disk that was thickest at the middle. The particles in the middle of the disk were under tremendous pressure. Temperatures rose until this central mass became white-hot and began to generate light and heat. In time this center part of the cloud became our sun, which continues to shine by nuclear fusion. Under very great pressure at very high temperatures, the nuclei of

119

hydrogen atoms fuse, forming the nuclei of helium atoms. As they do so, energy is given off. This energy is radiated by the sun.

While the sun was forming, the outer parts of the disc had broken up into whirlpools of gas and dust.

The dust particles settled toward the centers of the whirlpools. They began to collide. When two particles of the same size collided, they evaporated in the heat developed by the collision. When two particles of different sizes collided, the small one was added to the mass of the large one. In this way, during a few hundred million years, the planets formed. They were glowing hot, but they did not shine by nuclear fusion because their masses were not great enough to make the hydrogen nuclei fuse.

Each newborn planet was wrapped in a thick envelope of atmosphere. Radiation from the newly-glowing sun acted on the atmospheres, blowing away the lighter gases. The small planets near the sun lost much of the gas that surrounded them. Radiation from the sun was not so great in the case of the outer planets. Only a part of their atmospheres escaped.

Most scientists think that this theory is the best yet suggested. It leaves some questions unanswered. But it is in line with what is known about matter in the universe. And it does account for the pattern of the solar system. Born of the same spinning cloud, sun and planets would naturally form the pattern scientists have observed. The only exception is Pluto. But if Pluto was originally a satellite of Neptune, then it is less of a problem. The theory supposes that Neptune is the last of the true planets. Beyond it, where

The modern theory, based on Kant's ideas

121

the cloud was too thin for a planet to form, a vast swarm of comets may have taken shape.

This new theory has not been proved and may never be proved. Yet there is a good chance that we will one day have a better idea of whether or not it is true.

Scientists believe that new stars are constantly being formed. If they could watch stars forming, it would be like looking back five billion years to the time-misted beginnings of our own solar system.

Perhaps scientists can watch stars forming. Astronomers have found a number of dense, dark clouds in space. These clouds of gas and dust may be stars-in-the-making. Their birth may take a billion years. But watching even a tiny fraction of that time could provide clues to the beginning of our own solar system.

The same clues would help answer a second important question: do many stars have planets?

If planets are born of rare collisions between stars, then there can be only a few families of planets. But if planets are born along with stars, then there must be billions and billions of planets. And, scientists believe, life must exist on some of them.

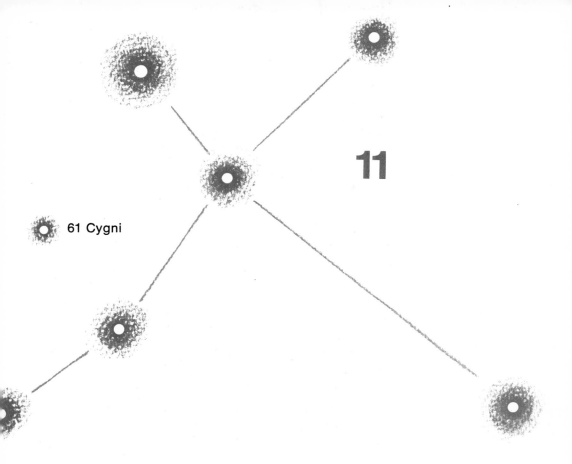

11

61 Cygni

Other Suns, Other Planets

In the constellation of Cygnus there is a star that astronomers have been watching with great interest. Its name is 61 Cygni, which means that it is the 61st star in its constellation.

This is a double star, consisting of two suns. And one of the suns has a companion that we cannot see. The companion circles its sun once every five years at a distance twice that of the earth from our sun. Though the companion cannot be seen, there is evidence it exists. The evidence is the wavy motion of one sun in the double star. Most astronomers think the invisible companion is a giant planet.

123

This clue—the wavy motion of certain stars—is the only sign that other solar systems may exist. For the stars are so distant that astronomers cannot hope to see whether or not they have planets. Even so, you would have a very hard time finding a scientist who thought that ours was the only solar system in the universe. Most scientists today believe that there are billions of families of planets. Many are convinced that life exists on a large number of those planets.

They reason this way:

The whole universe is built from the same elements. All matter, whether simple or complex, is built from these elements. And so far as is known, matter obeys the same laws in every part of the universe. The patterns in our small solar system are part of a pattern so big that the mind can hardly take it in.

We know that our sun was probably born of a cloud of dust and gas, along with its planets. Therefore it is reasonable to believe that other stars were born the same way and that they, too, have planets. And what we know about life on the earth seems to show that life will arise wherever the proper conditions exist.

The "proper conditions" are probably a sun like ours and a planet much like Earth.

Life requires a steady supply of heat and light. This condition rules out the close double stars, triple stars, and clusters of stars. Their planets would move in long orbits hostile to life. It rules out stars that flare up suddenly. In fact, it rules out every kind of star except those single stars that are as steady as ours.

Life requires just the right amount of the right kind

124

of atmosphere. So a life-supporting planet would have to be about the size and weight of Earth. A smaller planet loses its atmosphere; a bigger one may hold too much.

Finally, the planet would have to be just the right distance from its sun. This might be the earth's distance—or it might not. With a weaker sun, the planet would have to be closer. With a stronger one, it would have to be farther away.

Now, suppose that almost every star has a family of planets. How many might support life?

The astronomer first crosses out most of the families because they have the wrong kind of stars. (Perhaps half of the stars are doubles, triples, or clusters.) Within the remaining families, he crosses out most of the planets. They are either too close or too far from their suns. Of the planets left, he crosses out all those that are not about the size and weight of the earth. Finally, he points out that the right conditions do not necessarily mean that there is life on a planet. Life may not yet have begun. Or it may have ebbed away. Or the planet may always remain barren for reasons we do not understand.

Perhaps it begins to sound as if there are very few planets where life could exist. In a way, that is true. Life could exist on only a small percentage of the planets, perhaps one in a thousand or one in a million. But there are so many stars that this would still leave a huge number of planets on which life might exist. For the universe is constructed on so vast a scale that it staggers the imagination.

The stars you can see on a clear and moonless

125

Part of the Milky Way seen from the earth

night number little more than 2,000. They appear very numerous, but they are only a tiny handful of the stars revealed by a telescope. A small, inexpensive telescope shows you 100,000 stars. With the giant 200-inch telescope at Mount Palomar, astronomers can photograph more than a billion stars. And they estimate that in our galaxy alone there are billions and billions of stars.

Our galaxy is the Milky Way, which you know as a faintly glowing band that stretches across the night sky. To the ancient Greeks the band resembled a flow of milk. So they named it the *Galaxy,* which in English means the "Milky Way."

The faintly glowing band consists of stars—a vast multitude of distant stars. Yet it is only the starry edge of our galaxy. The complete Milky Way has the form of a spiral cloud. It includes the stars of our night sky. It includes our sun, which is simply one star in the galaxy. Dust clouds floating in space hide most of the galaxy. But astronomers see enough to know that it must contain about 100 billion stars.

126

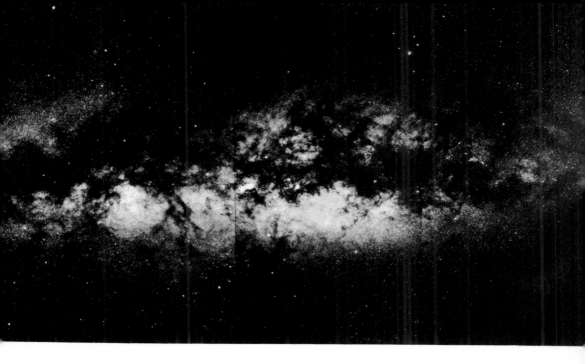

The billions of stars in our own galaxy are only the beginning of the stars in the universe. Some years ago, as telescopes were improving, astronomers found among the stars a number of faintly glowing shapes. Some were round, some oval; others were shaped something like a pinwheel. Astronomers called these **nebulae,** a Latin word for "clouds," because they believed the patches to be clouds of glowing gas. Then, as astronomers got better and better tools to work with, they discovered the truth. Some "nebulae" were not clouds of gas but clouds of stars. Each contained billions of stars and was a complete galaxy.

How many galaxies there are, no one knows. Astronomers estimate that within the range of the 200-inch telescope there are 100 million galaxies, each composed of billions of stars. And there is every reason to think that many more galaxies lie beyond the reach of the telescope.

The stars are so far away that astronomers cannot talk of their distances in miles. Instead they talk of **light-years.** A light-year is the distance that light

127

travels in a year. Since light moves at 186,000 miles a second, a light-year equals 5,880 billion miles.

Of all the stars, only our sun is less than a light-year away from us. The closest star other than the sun is Alpha Centauri, which is 4⅓ light-years away —about 25 trillion miles. Rigel, one of the bright stars in Orion, is 900 light-years away. The most distant stars we can see with the unaided eye are some 2,000 light-years away.

Still, compared with the "nebulae," the stars of the Milky Way are our close neighbors. Without a telescope, it is possible to see only one other galaxy, M 31, from the Northern Hemisphere. This galaxy is also called the Andromeda galaxy or nebula, because it looks as if it were in the constellation of Andromeda. It is more than 2 million light-years away from us. With the 200-inch telescope astronomers have seen galaxies more than 5 billion light-years away.

In view of these distances, it is no wonder that astronomers cannot see whether other stars have planets. Even if the star nearest us had a planet the size of Jupiter, it would be invisible.

The situation is tantalizing.

The universe may contain billions upon billions of planets where conditions are suitable for life. In the Milky Way alone there may be nearly 50 million families of planets. At least 100,000 of the families might contain planets where life could exist, and the figure may run much higher.

Yet the planets, if they exist, lie far beyond our vision. Reason and logic say they must exist. But we cannot see them.

128

Still, scientists feel sure that the planets are there, and many feel equally sure that these planets support some kind of life. What those kinds of life might be like, no one knows, for there is no reason to think that life elsewhere would have evolved along the same paths as life on Earth. Some scientists say we might not even recognize life forms on other planets. But other scientists feel so sure that intelligent life exists beyond our own planet that they have started to search for signs of it.

How can they search for life on planets that they cannot see and that may not exist? They can use giant radio telescopes to search for signals from intelligent life on other planets.

These scientists explain their search this way:

Suppose there is intelligent life on planets of other solar systems. Some of it will be as advanced as we are, or more advanced. The inhabitants of those planets will also be searching for life in other solar systems. They are probably beaming a message into space, hoping it will be received and answered.

The message would take the form of radio signals. The signals would be simple. But they would have a clearly artificial pattern so that they could be distinguished from other radio noise. For example, they might be based on prime numbers or simple arithmetic.

A few years ago United States astronomers began a search for such signals, turning their radio telescopes toward the stars that are nearest to us in space. This first search failed to discover any signals, but astronomers had known that their project was like

129

searching for a very small needle in a very big haystack. If we try, they had said, we may succeed or may fail. If we do not try, we are certain to fail.

Future searches may also fail. But even so, the day will almost certainly come when we know whether other stars have planets and life. The knowledge may well come through an invention as yet undreamed of, an invention which would be as important as the telescope.

If other solar systems exist, then men of Earth will seek to communicate with them and perhaps, one day, to visit them.

That day lies in the very distant future, for at present the stars are far beyond our grasp. With the kinds of rockets we now know, it would take 28,000 years to reach the nearest stars. To reach stars within a man's lifetime would require speeds comparable to that of light. The rockets we are developing will take us to the planets of our own solar systems, but not beyond.

For that reason, some people will tell you it is foolish to talk of reaching for the stars, trillions of miles away. Perhaps it is foolish. Perhaps it is a waste of time. But it does not seem so when you glance back at human history.

A hundred years ago, for example, men could not fly. They knew nothing of atomic energy. Electricity was a laboratory curiosity. And eight thousand years ago man was a wandering hunter who had not yet learned to use fire, tame animals, grow crops, or use metal.

History shows that man is an adventurer. He seeks

adventure in the exploration of both unknown lands and unknown ideas. He finds the means to explore by using his brain, the big forebrain that is unique to man among living things on Earth. His whole history has consisted of reaching for the "impossible," and attaining it.

Not long ago, a dreamer who wanted the impossible was said to be "reaching for the moon." Today the moon is within our grasp. And so, seeking other planets, we turn to the stars. They are far beyond our grasp, but in the light of human history it would be foolish not to reach. Even if we fail, we shall still do best with the stars as our goal.

Index

Page numbers in **bold face** are illustrations.

132

133

136